ANGELIC
PATHWAYS

About the Author

Chantel Lysette (Michigan) is an angel intuitive who has read for hundreds of clients and is the creator and host of "The Angel Gallery," a lecture/reading series. She is also a double certified Master of Usui Reiki, a form of intuitive energy healing. Lysette has appeared on *Coast to Coast AM* with George Noory, *Darkness Radio* with David Schrader, and other popular radio programs. Visit her online at ChantelLysette.com.

CHANTEL LYSETTE

ANGELIC
PATHWAYS

An Angel Medium's

Guide to Navigating

Our Human Experience

Llewellyn Publications
Woodbury, Minnesota

First Edition
First Printing, 2013

Book design by Donna Burch
Cover art: Clouds: BrandXPictures
           Feathers: iStockphoto.com/-Oxford-
Cover design by Ellen Lawson

Llewellyn Publications is a registered trademark of Llewellyn Worldwide Ltd.

Library of Congress Cataloging-in-Publication Data (Pending)
ISBN: 978-0-7387-3496-5

Llewellyn Worldwide Ltd. does not participate in, endorse, or have any authority or responsibility concerning private business transactions between our authors and the public.
  All mail addressed to the author is forwarded but the publisher cannot, unless specifically instructed by the author, give out an address or phone number.
  Any Internet references contained in this work are current at publication time, but the publisher cannot guarantee that a specific location will continue to be maintained. Please refer to the publisher's website for links to authors' websites and other sources.

Llewellyn Publications
A Division of Llewellyn Worldwide, Ltd.
2143 Wooddale Drive
Woodbury, MN 55125-2989
www.llewellyn.com

Printed in the United States of America

Other Books by Chantel Lysette

Azrael Loves Chocolate, Michael's A Jock
(Llewellyn, 2008)

The Angel Code
(Llewellyn, 2010)

For Jake

Contents

This chapter explores Chantel's background and experience with connecting to the Realm of Spirit and
engaging the archangels.

Chapter 2 offers an intimate look at the archangels as
well as a detailed account of the human soul's existence in the Realm of Spirit and how each soul begins
its journey to the human world.

Chapter 3 presents detailed accounts of real-life interactions with the archangels and how life lessons are
utilized to facilitate the growth and evolution of the
soul while existing in the human world.

Chapter 4 covers the death process and a soul's journey back to the Realm of Spirit.

This chapter is a candid update on Chantel's painful
journey out of the dire life circumstances mentioned
throughout the book and the beginning of life anew.

Acknowledgments

I thank God and his heavenly archangels for putting up with me and my stubborn ways. I could not have made it this far without them.

My deepest gratitude goes to Llewellyn Publications and my cherished readers for their continued support.

PREFACE

While convalescing after having a stroke in 2004, I found myself at the lowest point of my life. I had lost my house, my car, and my savings. I had lost everything I owned. And to seemingly make me a new poster child for the book of Job, friends and what little family I had walked out of my life right when I needed them most.

Paralyzed and penniless, I had no one.

Months before the stroke, I had left a job of seven years. It was a stressful daily grind that had landed me in the hospital twice with a life-threatening condition. But because I was young (not yet thirty), I thought I would bounce back.

I was wrong. My health was on a steady decline, and when I wound up in the hospital in need of emergency surgery—only to have my employer show up with work and my laptop for me to complete projects in bed—I knew something had to change. What that change would be, I hadn't a clue.

After countless hours of prayer, Gabriel came to me and instructed me to simply leave the job. While that seemed to be the logical thing to do, being as it was slowly killing me, it wasn't practical. I owned my house and had car and college loans to pay off. Sure, I had my savings, but that would have lasted me only six months if I were unemployed—and provided I didn't run into another crisis.

After much internal struggle, I finally surrendered and left my job in search of less stressful employment. It was then when Gabriel and I began to lock horns. He insisted I not look for work, while I insisted that it was the smart, proactive thing to do.

Who is Gabriel? Well, he's an archangel. And yes, I mean *the* Archangel Gabriel—angel of the Annunciation and messenger of messengers. As an intuitive and angel medium, I've been actively engaging the benevolent Hosts of Heaven for nearly twenty years. When I first encountered them, I thought what any sane person would think: *Oh God, I'm losing my mind*. But the angels have proven they are very real and very tangible not simply by bestowing upon me wisdom and insight, but by the accuracy of the information they have provided. One might say that an accurate prediction here and there could be a coincidence, but when I began to connect with the angels, I was seeing signs and miracles nearly every day of my life. That might make one think that I was welcoming and accepting of their divine presence or that I was ecstatic to have been chosen to deliver their messages.

That notion couldn't be further from the truth.

To this day, I still play tug of war with the angels whenever they bring to me a nugget of wisdom or a vision of the future. There is still a part of me that continues to test the validity of our intercommunication, not because I don't believe in them, but because I'm human and must filter their messages through my own thoughts, feelings, and personal desires.

As you'll soon read, accepting the angels into my life was one of the most difficult transitions I had to endure. Correction: I'm still going through that transition, but I would be remiss to deny how much I've grown spiritually over the years with the careful, compassionate nurturing of the archangels. I'm almost ashamed of what I've put them through in the process. Almost.

But, angels are angels for a reason. They can take a beating from us humans and not even blink. They're used to being emotional punching bags for us, and Heaven knows they have been for me. But in my defense, to get me where they wanted me as a medium whose focus is more on helping others to connect to the divine than offering predictions, the angels had to break me down and rebuild me. They had to bring my life as I knew it to an end and then force me to start anew.

I've said it many times in my lectures, consultations, and books, and I'll say it again: *I'm not a fortuneteller!* I'm not the type of medium who will stand in a packed auditorium and tell you that your Aunt Phyllis said hello, nor do I have winning lottery numbers or know if or when you'll launch your dream career. My job is to connect you to your angels and spirit guides so you can learn directly from them that which will help you to grow and mature spiritually. One could say that my job is to make my own job obsolete, being as my purpose is not to hold someone's hand and guide them through life with a prediction every week, but to train others to connect to their own guides so my presence isn't even required.

There's no need for a middleman when it comes to paving your path into the future. Firstly, the future is already set. Secondly, the archangels are already available to you and ready to connect in order to guide you along that path.

Everyone has the capacity to connect to the divine, but everyone's gift is different. More importantly, the experiences that help you to hone your gifts will be countless and varying, and so it is for you that I have written this book. I seek to share with you more than information on the gifts of intuition, the angels, Heaven, what occurs before we're born, and what transpires when we die. I want to share with you my own personal experiences so that they serve as examples of each and every facet of spirituality covered in this book. Woven in between these pages is the story of a spirit on a human journey from Heaven and back as guided by the hands of God, the hands of fate.

As I've expressed in my previous books, I cannot be emphatic enough when I say that our connection to the divine is a connection we all should strive to develop and nurture. Such a connection helps us to navigate life and understand the purpose and meaning in everything. I would never tell you or anyone, however, that making the connection will make your life easier. On the contrary, the more spiritual growth you experience, the tougher the challenges you'll face. But in turn, those challenges will facilitate even more spiritual growth. Sometimes it's easy for me to say that, but there have been times—as you will read throughout this book—when I've had very human moments and wanted nothing to do with the angels or spiritual growth, for oftentimes growth brings change, and change isn't always comfortable.

For me, change was downright unbearable at times, but the angels dragged me through it kicking and screaming. Thankfully, on the other side of it all was clarity, as well as a better understanding of myself, this world, and worlds unseen.

———————————— ❧ ————————————

"The career that is coming to you does not require a resumé," he said to me one night as I fervently folded fancy linen stationery with my resumé and cover letter printed on it. In between licking envelopes and sticking stamps on them, I cursed Gabriel for luring me into a situation that now seemed more stressful than the job I once had. At least with the job, I had a paycheck every Friday. Now, I was facing debt faster than I had anticipated because I had foolishly neglected to consider my COBRA payments when I resigned. They were five hundred dollars a month.

After two months of tangling and tussling with the archangel over searching for employment, he finally won. I returned home one summer Sunday evening from church and a luncheon with friends. And then I collapsed.

Three days later, I woke up paralyzed in the hospital.

Three months later, I was throwing thirty years of my life into industrial-size garbage bags and heaving them into a car in order to keep my belongings from being set out on the curb. I had lost ownership of my house. Friends I had talked to every week stopped calling. The one family member I thought

I could trust labeled me as a financial liability and disowned me so fast, it left me dizzy.

After watching one person after another abandon me, I expected kindness from no one. But before I was set out on the streets like discarded rubbish, a family took me in, and it was in a ten-by-ten room that I would lie and stare at the ceiling for weeks, months ... years, all the while cursing Gabriel and every other angel in Heaven. Yes, I cursed God quite a few times, too, despite the fact that at least I wasn't in a homeless shelter ... yet.

I wanted to die. And I was so furious with God over Gabriel's seeming betrayal that I didn't even care if I went to Hell, too.

Needless to say, I wanted nothing to do with the angels ever again, but they are a persistent lot. Archangel Raphael, the angel of healing, remained close, and Gabriel offered words of wisdom, but nothing provided solace. Nothing could quell my anguish.

"Hold on, Chantel. Be patient," Archangel Raphael would whisper as I wept ceaselessly.

"Do you think we would bring you this far to let you falter?" Gabriel said one night, to which I responded, "If I hadn't listened to you, I wouldn't be in this situation!"

"Yes, you would have," his voice was firm. "All of this is a part of God's plan. All of it."

"Well, let me tell you where you can stick *God's plan* ..."

But then another angel came into the fray, Archangel Michael, chief archangel and Heaven's master general. One might think that he was sent in to bring me to heel and press me into listening to God's messengers, but no. He brought with him a bright smile and a sense of humor that was able to crack through the wall of angst I had built around myself while wallowing in total poverty and utter solitude. It was a loneliness so profound that I often found myself picking up my cell phone to make sure it was working. No one called. And no one came.

No one, save the angels.

Slowly, Michael's charm and gentleness wore me down, and I became a bit more receptive to God's messengers again, but not by much. Still, my doubt in Heaven lingered as the dark clouds of uncertainty loomed low over my head every single waking hour. I was hearing the angels' messages, but I refused to listen. What they had to say seemed like all the wrong answers to my unending barrage of questions as to why my life had taken such a harrowing turn for the worse.

All Raphael had to offer was, "This too shall pass," while Gabriel and Michael harped on about God's plan and how my circumstances were meant to be. After a while, it became far too easy to tune the angels out. I had gotten to a point in my life where all I expected was misery anyway—misery with a heaping side of mistrust in God and in my psychic ability to hear him and his messengers.

And so, it hardly surprised me that my health took another nosedive in 2006.

This time it was pneumonia.

I felt so ill the first night that I thought I was having a heart attack. The chest pains started around two AM, and my spirit was so downtrodden that I didn't even bother calling for an ambulance. I merely sat up, wrote out my will, and then lay back down to wait for death to come.

When the light of dawn seeped into my room from beneath my door, I was disappointed that I was still alive, angry even. Angry and indignant. But I was in unbearable pain as well, and that motivated me to finally go to the hospital, where I was admitted for three days. I cursed in frustration because at the time I had no medical insurance. I knew I would incur a medical bill so huge that it would surely follow me into the afterlife.

Since I was still suffering from complications from the stroke, excruciating pain had become the norm for me, and it was even more so because I was now in a hospital bed without all the blankets and pillows I normally used just to make lying down somewhat bearable. By time I was admitted, I was sobbing and begging for someone to put me out of my misery. That's when the physician ordered heavy-duty pain medications so I could at least sleep.

And there, on the third night around three in the morning, I lay in bed staring at the crucifix on my hospital room wall. A patient in the adjacent room was blasting Mass on her television as loudly as if it were three in the afternoon. I assumed she was elderly, partially deaf, or both. And even though I'm not Catholic, I still listened intently and welcomed the soothing voices of the priest, choir, and congregation. It brought me a bit of peace that night. Well, that and the morphine.

As I lay there quietly drifting back and forth between self-pity and apathy, like a rowboat in breezy waters, Archangel Michael strolled into my room. Glorious and beautiful, charming and sweet, he walked like he owned the place. It was a slow, confident lope that commanded attention and perhaps even admiration. This archangel is not bad on the eyes, to say the least.

Gathering his white robes, he sat on the side of my bed and chuckled at me with his usual lopsided grin.

"What's so funny?" Even to my own ears, my voice was thick with the effects of pain medication.

"Do you know how difficult it is to talk to you when you're on that stuff?" He leveled his eyes at me. When I was in the hospital for two months after the stroke, I had my first experience with morphine. As someone who didn't even take Tylenol before all this happened, my tolerance for the drug was ultra low. And though it didn't tune out the angels, it did ease me into not giving a damn about anything they or God had to say.

"Well, good lookin'," I giggled back, "apparently it's not that difficult. We're talkin' now, aren't we?"

With a knowing smirk, the sun-kissed angel nodded, his piercing eyes bright with mirth. "That's 'cause I'm making sure you remember this."

"I don't get it, Mike," I sighed in defeat. "Why this? Why now? I'm down to one can of food and I have eight dollars left to my name. I can't afford a ten-thousand-dollar hospital bill." Earlier that day, a hospital representative from the billing department had come to visit me. With a clipboard in hand, he gazed at me with cold, scrutinizing eyes.

"Our records show that you didn't list any medical insurance," he said as he stood just inside the door. He kept his distance as if I had been diagnosed with some type of flesh-eating plague. "We were wondering how you intend to cover the bill for this stay." I had to give him credit—at least he went straight to the point. He didn't even bother to say hello.

I shifted in the bed with a grimace of pain and cursed under my breath as I tried to get comfortable. I then looked up at him with an equally cold gaze. "I own nothing. I have no house, no car, and no assets. For the most part, you can consider me homeless." And that was the truth. Though I was not houseless (because I was living under a roof), I was homeless. I was living at a place where I wasn't really welcome, not even during holidays. So, yes, I was very much *homeless*. To say otherwise would be like saying that a person wasn't homeless because they were living in a shelter.

The man's expression hardened as his eyes narrowed. I, however, didn't so much as blink. And then, seemingly without a breath, he turned on his heels and left with a curt "thank you." The visit had only made real what I had been dreading since I had been admitted: I was going to wind up with a bill I couldn't pay. Great. I could add it to the already growing pile of bills that had gone into default. *Take a number and get in line*, I mentally projected to the man as I drew my hands over my face in weariness and hopeless resignation.

And now, here Michael was paying me a visit some twelve hours later. His disposition was the polar opposite of the billing rep, his presence was warm and comforting. With his eyes aglow with pure love and compassion, the archangel leaned over and kissed me tenderly on the forehead. "Tomorrow morning you'll understand why you're here."

"And?"

"And hopefully the flood of doubt you've been wading in all this time will ebb, kid. Get some sleep." With that, he vanished.

The next day, the hospital was ready to release me. No doubt, they weren't willing to keep me an hour more than the law absolutely required them to. And though I was more than happy to know that the time meter on my bed would cease racking up fees faster than a New York taxicab, a sense of dread seeped into my soul as I thought of what I'd be returning to—a dark room full of loneliness, isolation, and hunger.

I had never in my short years encountered money problems of this magnitude. My parents had been determined and dedicated workers who did everything they could to put me through school. Adopting their work ethic, I got a job when I was thirteen and worked every summer thereafter. Once in high school, I also worked after school and on the weekends. So as a kid, I never really knew what "going without" was like. To be suddenly hit with that reality in my adult life was more than a rude awakening. It was raw, agonizing torment not unlike what I imagine would be the equivalent of being set upon by a swarm of soul-eating demons. And since it was caused by things I couldn't control—a massive health crisis with no end in sight—I felt that it was an outright cruel and unusual punishment from God.

Then there was one of the most painful notions of all: if I had died right then and there, I would have done so penniless and without so much as even an insurance policy to cover burial costs. The thought of being a nameless body in a pine box, *if* I even made it that far, washed over me like ice water. Without friends or family, there would have been no one to even check to see that I hadn't been chopped up and sold on the black market for whatever usable body parts I had left. Still, one unbearable truth remained: I had tumbled gracelessly from the status of the contented middle class to that of the faceless, voiceless impoverished.

Unable to stand the shame and humiliation a minute longer, the dam of my emotions crumbled and I broke into heaving sobs, screaming at the injustice of it all.

Just then, the nurse who was charged with the task of releasing me entered the room with paperwork. I was weeping so hard, I couldn't breathe, couldn't talk. Without a word, she sat on the bed and put her hand upon my shoulder; and after another moment, I finally regained enough dignity to stop my tears and look up into her eyes.

Her gaze nearly stole my breath away. They were the eyes of an angel. She seemed to have so much of Michael's spirit in her that I wondered if I had finally cracked and was hallucinating.

"You know," she began, "today was supposed to be my day off. And I could have turned them down when they called me to come in, but something said I needed to be here today."

"Michael," I barely uttered.

"Pardon?" She then looked down at her hospital ID and corrected me: "Michelle." She thought I had misread her name, but I was simply addressing the light I saw in her eyes.

"No," I said politely. "The Archangel Michael is all around you."

The color drained from the nurse's face and she nervously pushed her blonde hair back out of her eyes.

"Come again?"

"I see angels, and you have a lot of Archangel Michael with you." I knew how much of a lunatic I sounded right then and there, but what did I have to lose? If they stuck me in the mental ward, at least I would have three meals a day. Not to mention, fellow patients would be vastly more entertaining than counting the dots on the tacky, yellowed wallpaper in the room back at the house.

Nervously, Michelle fumbled with my release papers and cleared her throat. "I know. I love Archangel Michael very much. I think he's always been with me, ever since I was a child. I even named my son after him." She took a cleansing breath as her concerned, pensive eyes looked me over. "What's troubling you so deeply today?"

My tears immediately began again. "It's too long a story," I sighed and then looked at the wall. "All I know is when I leave here today, I have one can of ravioli left that I can heat on my desk lamp and eight dollars in my pocket.

"In light of my current circumstances, I've recently become a proponent of euthanasia," I continued as I tapped my chin. "So I'm willing to volunteer if you think the hospital will do it for free." My pride was decimated. Years prior, I would have rather died than admit to such problems, such utter failures.

"Those are harsh words for someone who can see angels," the nurse shot back quickly.

"You think I'm nuts, don't you?"

"For seeing angels? No. For wanting to die when they're so obviously close to you? Yes." With that, she got up to fetch me a box of tissues and then left the room. When she returned, I had dried my tears and regrouped a bit more. But I felt smaller than ever, and I was furious with myself for unloading all my woes into the lap of a complete stranger.

My sense of dignity, it seemed, had flown out the hospital's third-floor window.

"When you get home, make sure you look in the release packet I gave you. There's something very important in there you need to see," she said as she wheeled me down to the hospital entrance.

"A bill?" I asked dryly.

"No, just a little something from a mutual friend," she chirped.

I couldn't help my cynical and incredulous chuckle. "Michael told me that this morning I'd find out why I came down with pneumonia."

"Well, the angels always keep their promises."

"Yeah, I know," I sighed contritely. She helped me into a taxi and I was back to my place of residence all too quickly. Once I got settled into my room, I finally opened the folder and inside was a small get-well card—and a check for five hundred dollars.

I held the check in my trembling hands for what seemed like hours as I pondered her note:

My son, Michael, is going through a very difficult time right now. He's young and looking for answers in all the wrong places. I trust that you can see the angels and talk to them, and I believe that Archangel Michael sent you to me today, as no one has ever said to me what you did. There's no way you could have known what I've held in my heart without some connection to him, so I thank you for being so brave to speak up. If I may, I must ask one small favor. Please talk to

Archangel Michael for me and ask him how I can best guide my son off the path of destruction he's on.

I immediately called out to the archangel, who then showed up with a soft smile.

"Thank you." I flashed the check up at him, as I felt rather sheepish for having doubted him.

"Don't thank me. Next time you get caught in a flood of doubt and you begin to wonder if we're here for you or not, let today's experience serve as your life preserver."

I nodded, surrendering to his wisdom. "So what about Michelle's son?"

"Grab your notebook and pen, kid. This is gonna be a long dictation."

I didn't hesitate to get a response mailed back to Michelle, who replied two months later expressing that everything Archangel Michael had instructed had worked. She also sent another check for two hundred fifty dollars.

Any other time, my pride would have made me send both checks back, but hunger and desperation, I have found, trump pride every time.

Most of the money went toward groceries. What I had left over went toward repairing my clunker of a laptop so I could access my old manuscripts and start writing after years of doing nothing with my life but participate in daily pity parties.

Doing so would eventually lead to the sale of my first book, *Azrael Loves Chocolate, Michael's A Jock*.

And so here I am.

Michelle and I never connected again beyond the second letter, but it was meant to be. My winding up in the hospital with pneumonia was never about the money. It was about trusting in God and understanding that all challenges that come before us occur for a reason. The hospital visit was as much about Michelle finding guidance for her son as it was about my regaining trust in the guidance of God's messengers.

It also taught me a difficult lesson in how the universe sometimes works. There will be moments in our lives when prayers aren't answered with rainbows and daffodils. Sometimes they're answered with storm clouds and downpours, but the angels will always be there with an umbrella, a raft, and a helping hand.

So when the flood waters of challenges, disappointments, and doubt begin to rise, don't flail and try to fight the deluge. Fatigue and panic will only cause you to get pulled down by the undertow. Instead, clutch onto the guiding hands of God and his heavenly messengers and let them pull you through. They're awesome swimmers and they make the perfect flotation devices.

chapter one

THE "GIFT" OF INTUITION

Since the release of my two books, *Azrael Loves Chocolate, Michael's A Jock* and *The Angel Code*, I've been inundated with e-mails all expressing the same sentiment: *Gee, I wish I could communicate with the angels the way you seem to, Chantel! It must make life infinitely easier to deal with.* And after I'm done holding my aching sides from laughing so hard, I usually reply, "Working with the angels has been *anything* but a walk in the park."

As more and more readers discover my work, they quickly realize what sets me apart from most of the other angel mediums out there—I don't sugarcoat divinity. While connecting with the divine is often awe-inspiring, uplifting, and encouraging, it also has a side that sometimes makes me want to scream, pound the walls, and shake my fists in frustration.

―――――――――― ❧ ――――――――――

From the very start when I began connecting to the spiritual world, I faced trials and challenges that would make a seasoned military veteran shudder with thoughts of his first days at boot camp. Learning to trust in my intuitive gifts proved just as grueling as learning to use them. And as if those in the Realm of Spirit possessed nothing less than the sickest, cruelest sense of humor, a spirit guide—not an angel—was assigned to me for *practice*. I'm sure he would say it was more like target practice.

Poor Jake. When he was first sent to me, he had returned to the Realm of Spirit only a year prior. It was 1993 when he died in a tragic accident in the prime of his life. And, as if it wasn't torture enough to be pulled away from his happy life so abruptly, a year later he wound up serving as a spiritual and emotional punching bag for an ungrateful, thick-headed, would-be psychic medium. Me.

The night I first met him, the sky was falling. Thunder rumbled in the distance as evening shoppers ran from storefronts through a flooding parking lot to their cars. There were a few of us, however, who stood oblivious to the downpour and the crackling lightning overhead as we gazed enamored into the window of a candlelit storefront. I stood with my nose pressed to the window as condensation diffused the light of the candles inside. Then, as if suddenly waking from a dream, I shook off my rain-curtained gaze, wove through the other onlookers, and entered the store.

Despite the white candles lit about, the store was quite dark, which only magnified the eerie, foreboding silence. Creep factor aside, the store seemed to be an innocuous, albeit eccentric, gift and novelty shop. I strolled down the aisles of games, puzzles, and gadgets—*Nothing special there,*

I thought. Nothing really caught my eye until I glanced at the back of the store where the poster display stood. I wasn't sure why I was drawn there, but my steps were quick and purposeful as I obeyed my intuition and curiosity.

Eagerly, I flipped through the posters, seeing nothing of great interest at first. But then one almost got by me. It was an image of a handsome young man. Crow-black hair fell in his eyes as he bowed his head, chin to chest. In fact, the sweat-laden strands hid his face completely and fell upon burnished shoulders. No, this wasn't some generic, high-gloss beach boy sporting a tan and other wares for girls to drool over. Instead of a blue sky, white sands, and a frothing ocean as a backdrop, there was only an ominous orange glow.

An immediate feeling of great unease came over me as my eyes took in the life-size poster. It was then when I heard the sounds of rattling chains. Frightened and confused, I took a step back only to be startled by the sudden, piercing sound of a soul-shattering scream. I yelped and tripped over my own feet as I backed up against the wall, but I couldn't take my eyes off the poster. I couldn't even blink as the image commanded my gaze. It wasn't a difficult feat after all, for what was at one moment a mere photo then became a vision, a window into another reality. The dim, orange light reflecting on the man's torso began to dance and flicker as if unseen flames were its source. As I felt a blast of immense heat assault me from the poster's direction, I had no doubt that somewhere in the background a fire was raging.

I reached out my hand toward the image when I noticed that the man's chest was sharply rising and falling. He was heaving for air as if he'd just run a marathon, and I imagined that the unbearable heat was hardly helping his situation. His suffering and obvious distress drew me in, triggering an overwhelming desire to help. It was at that moment that my intuition told me if I could touch his heart, I could rescue this tortured soul from his nightmare.

When my fingers were mere centimeters from his chest, his head shot up and his anguished eyes pierced me like a lance. Pain was etched deep in his sharp features as he tried to catch his breath. Sweat matted his hair and rolled down the sides of his face, and for what seemed like an eternity, our gazes remained locked.

My concentration was finally broken when he flinched—whether it was from pain or from some ghastly sight beyond my limited vision, I wasn't sure. Regardless, I knew that he was struggling to break free from whatever was holding him captive. Though the poster only depicted him from the waist up, I could discern by how tightly his arms were drawn in before him that he had been bound at the wrists. Compulsion to help, be damned. A fear of what I had stumbled upon, and what my tampering might unleash, won out. I slowly began to retreat.

"Guilt … regret," he finally said, stopping me in my tracks. "It's too much to bear. No one should have to endure this. No one, Chantel. Not even you. You don't want this." He choked on a sob as tears streaked his soot-stained cheeks.

"Jake," I breathed as I cowered against the wall; his name had suddenly popped into my head. "I don't know how to help you."

His eyes lifted heavenward for a brief moment as the chains rattled ominously again, then he let out a bloodcurdling wail of pure, concentrated agony: "You don't want this!"

––––––––––––––––––––––– ❦ –––––––––––––––––––––––

"Jake!" I awoke, clutching my blankets and shaking. I could have sworn I had screamed his name aloud, but my friend, who was sleeping right beside me during a girls' sleepover, didn't stir. I tried to push Jake's tormented face from my mind, but there was a strange allure about him—and the dream itself—that held my imagination in thrall.

It was 1994. I was in college, in debt, and completely disenchanted with life, so I found the dream a vexing, albeit welcomed, distraction from the mundane. I spent weeks pondering its meaning. My angel with the crow-black hair seemed more like a demon at first, coming to shake my rickety spiritual life into a pile of rubble. Was this dream predicting a hell-to-come for me? I didn't know. Perhaps it was more foretelling of a hell-to-come for Jake, as I would probably be one of the most difficult-to-convince humans ever encountered by a spirit guide.

At the time, I didn't know exactly who Jake was, and for all I did know, he was simply a bogeyman that haunted all of my dreams and stood in the shadowy corners of my bedroom daring me to fall asleep. I tried my best to ignore his presence, or at least what I considered a presence. Though he often spoke to me in dreams, and I could only later vaguely recall his words, I was convinced that he was yet another figment of my overactive imagination.

For two years Jake haunted me in my sleep, until one rainy night in 1996 when he finally stepped outside the parameters of dreamscape and into my reality.

I was in a rare mood that night, hypersensitive to the world around me. I had been this way before, and it was annoying as hell. My senses were acutely aware of the smallest things. Eating was difficult—processed foods had a toxic taste, and the metallic taste in red meat was more than I could stomach. I couldn't tolerate the faintest of whispers without getting a headache. And if my father had left an appliance on somewhere in the house, I could actually hear the buzzing of its electrical currents.

Visually, I was sensitive to light. But even as I sat in the darkness, light danced before my eyes, either in the form of bright flashes; rapid, streaming colors; or slow, colorful flows like something in a lava lamp. There was no escaping it. Even with my eyes shut tight, I could not gain the peace of total darkness.

All of that, on top of what I knew were nothing more than anxiety attacks, left me feeling stressed and clawing at the walls. It also didn't help that I was coming down from a conversation I'd had that day with some college friends. We were all feeling as if we were trapped in limbo as we faced graduation without a clue of what we wanted to do with our lives. There was this sense of being lost and running against the clock to … nowhere. We had come to the painful conclusion that life no longer held any magic or meaning. Gone was the innocence of childhood. Gone were the hopes and dreams of doing anything truly meaningful in life. Here we were, all stuck in jobs none of us wanted with the realization that we were quickly becoming our parents, living only to pay the bills and nothing more.

With those thoughts still fresh in my mind, I sat alone that night in the silence and refuge of the family room and listened as a thunderstorm slowly moved in from the distance. I tried to think about other, more positive things, but instead my brain ceaselessly churned on the negative cycle. I knew if I didn't find a diversion quickly, I would go nuts. Still, the thought of turning on the television, with all its light and noise, made me physically ill.

After a few more minutes of mental torture, I began to weep. I was so afraid of facing the world with no sense of direction. It was a world that seemed so broken with its many problems.

This is not the life I signed up for, I thought as I clutched my hair in frustration and tried not to give in to the notion that there was nothing truly worth pursuing in life. At twenty-three years old, I was already angry, tired, and jaded. I'd seen all too many times just how unfair life was—to everyone. No one seemed to be happy. Everyone seemed to be clambering over everyone else to get ahead, no matter how it affected others. In what I then considered the muck and mire of humanity, I could see very little love or compassion; and those few souls who still managed to retain a bit of love in their hearts were often crushed under the heels of those driven by nefarious ambitions.

"My God," I groaned hoarsely, "what's the point?"

It was at that moment I heard a whisper. I thought it was my father calling from upstairs. Clearing my throat, I replied and waited for what I knew would be a request for a glass of juice. But there was nothing. I called to my father again. Still nothing. I sighed.

"Chantel," I heard the masculine voice repeat in the darkness, and I knew then that it was not the voice of my father. A frost crept over my skin, and the hairs on my arms stood at attention. Gripped by fear, I wiped my tears away and slowly brought my feet up upon the couch. My only defense was a single pillow.

Of course I entertained the possibility that sanity had finally left me and that a trip to the state mental hospital was due first thing in the morning. And I knew that if I answered the voice, I would probably hear something I would regret. Was it a demon or devil coming to tempt me to Hell?

"Who's there?" I asked, my voice muffled behind the pillow. I was frozen to that couch but not so frozen that I couldn't bolt through a window if objects went flying through the air. After all, I'm a child of the eighties; I grew up watching films like *Poltergeist* and *The Amityville Horror*. I was mentally prepared to run as if my pantyhose were on fire, and, unlike in the horror movies, I wouldn't look back or trip over a paperclip in the middle of the street.

"Chantel, please don't be afraid of me. I'm only here to help."

"Yeah … right."

Help me how? was the big question. Jake never provided a verbal answer; instead, he spoke through his actions in the coming months.

Initially, his guidance seemed innocuous enough. He proved himself to be a huge boon at work by helping me stay one step ahead of a manager who excelled at procrastination.

"Don't plan on leaving work on time tonight," Jake said, sitting cross-legged in one of my office chairs.

"Wha ...?" I looked up, just as I was starting to pack my briefcase, to see my boss pass my door, then backtrack into my office with a stupid grin.

"Oh, Chantel, you're still here! Good."

"Told you," Jake whispered. Because I often worked late, well past midnight after coming in at ten AM, the night watchman and I were the only two left in the sprawling complex. To make matters worse, I was always parked in the dark, secluded lot a block away and well out of anyone's earshot. I worked in an affluent neighborhood where crime was nil, but still, one couldn't be too careful, and it was during those moments when I clung to Jake the tightest.

"You're fine," he'd whisper. "I would never lead you into harm's way, Chantel. There's no one out here but you, me, the trees, and a few ghosts who couldn't care less about us." *Ghosts? Great. Just great.* It was no secret that the century-old complex where I worked was haunted. Employees, patrons, and even contractors had reported seeing strange shadows, moving furniture, and doors that opened and closed by themselves. They had also heard voices, whispers, and footsteps when there was no one else around.

Many of the employees made sure to be out of there before sundown if possible. The night watchman, however, seemed to love his job because of the strange things he'd seen. In fact, it was he who turned me on to the late-night radio show *Coast to Coast AM*. At two in the morning, I'd be folding letters at the front desk while he and Jake sat back and listened to the show that covered everything and anything paranormal.

The funniest late-night moments I recall were times when a ghost expert or psychic medium was on the radio discussing the afterlife. Jake would just sit there and shake his head in pity.

"What a crock of…" he'd moan and roll his eyes, making me giggle. But his scoffing made me realize what I truly had in my presence. He wasn't some ghost, someone who had refused to walk into the Light. He was someone who had lived, gone to Heaven, and returned to help us hapless humans along. Don't get me wrong—I begged him numerous times to push a pen off my desk or change the channel on my television set.

His usual comeback: "My days in theater are over."

Or were they?

Other than begging that I accept his presence in my life, Jake had but one other request.

"Write my story," he would frequently whisper. "Please, Chantel." His voice seemed so pain-filled that I couldn't help but feel guilty that I used the excuse of my two part-time jobs, school, and Goth club hopping to avoid doing so. The man was relentless, but after a while, I told him I wasn't familiar with the medium he wanted me to use. He had wanted me to write a screenplay, and I didn't even know that's what movie scripts were called, much less how to write one.

"I'll teach you," he said. I was hesitant. Here this spirit guide was bonding with me and establishing waking-world contact with me. Why me, of all the billions of people in the world? To this day, I still don't know. All I do know is that the more he pressed me, the more I reverted back to how I was when he first spoke to me that night from the dining room—wary as hell. If I was going to make a sacrifice of time for him, darn it all, I had every intention of putting him through a gauntlet of spiritual challenges, including a homemade exorcism that I had learned from a book at the university library. I mean, I had to do something before I committed to him. Wouldn't *you* after first seeing him as an inmate of some infernal prison in a dream?

As our relationship progressed, I became more unbearable than ever. Neurotic, even. One day I was accusing him of being a demon come to tempt me away from God, and the next I was questioning my sanity since I was not only hearing a disembodied voice, I was *arguing* with it. Worse yet, I could see Jake in my intuitive vision—my third eye—although I didn't actually realize I *was* seeing him. I thought I was imagining him, visualizing him. But when it finally dawned on me that I could see him as easily as I could see any corporeal human, I only felt kookier. My life was starting to look like a Goth version of the movie *Drop Dead Fred*, only Jake was a lot cooler and didn't cause me to do things that got me in trouble... often.

The biggest argument we ever had occurred around the first anniversary of his contacting me on that memorable night in 1996. The project he had seemed so desperate for me to complete was done. My screenplay won multiple awards at the university, but when I attempted to get it made into a movie, I unwittingly allowed the script to be stolen right out from under me. When I realized that all my hard work had been claimed by someone else, I was pissed off to a level of monumental proportions. I was angry at the thieves, the situation, the fact that I could do nothing to bring them to justice and the fact that Jake had even allowed the theft to occur. He had actually served as my mentor and muse for the entire piece! It was what I then considered my most creative moment ever. I blamed him for allowing my hard work and research to go to waste.

"Jake, go! I never want to see you again!" I screamed as I paced my bedroom like a caged lioness. "I hope you enjoyed your little game with me. You're nothing but a damned devil, so go back to Hell where you came from." Jake hadn't said a word in his own defense. He merely nodded respectfully and vanished. I can only liken the feeling he left behind to that of total emptiness. Where there was warmth, peace, and security was now nothing. Absolutely nothing.

As the hours passed, I warred with myself. Part of me wanted to call him back to my side and apologize for berating him so mercilessly. The other part of me was still wondering if he was just some ghost having a laugh at my expense. Upon nightfall, I decided it was best that I move on without him. After all, it was through his influence and urging that I had missed what I then thought was the opportunity of a lifetime.

The next morning, I got up for work still feeling as angry as ever. My fury at Jake was still off the charts, and all I wanted was to go back to the time before he came into my life. I had gotten so used to talking to him almost every morning before work that even sunny days without him seemed bleak. This particular morning, however, I was determined to start anew. I thought putting on a new suit and creating a new hairdo would make me feel better.

Convinced the makeover had done the trick, I headed to work with a new attitude. But somewhere between matching accessories and trying on a new perfume, I left my brain on the dresser, for upon getting in the car, I decided not to wear my seatbelt lest I wrinkle my new suit. Instead, I decided to drive a bit more carefully.

"Good morning." Jake appeared from nowhere, as I sat in the usual rush-hour traffic. Whenever I was driving, he always appeared sitting in the center of the back seat.

"I told you to go away and stay gone."

"Put your seatbelt on," he said calmly.

"Leave me alone, Jake. Go. Away."

"Put your seatbelt on right now and I promise I'll leave."

"Fine," I grumbled and clicked the belt in place. I looked up in the rearview mirror, scowling at him. "Happy now?"

"Actually, yes. Thank you," he replied, and that's when I looked past him—or more like *through* him—and saw a car speeding toward me.

It wasn't stopping.

I gripped the wheel tighter, held my breath, and braced myself as I heard a symphony of screeching tires on the road behind me, followed by the thunderous roar of metal impacting metal.

I walked away from the collision with only whiplash. My poor Chevy wasn't so lucky, as the impact had slammed my car into the one ahead of me. So much for my new attitude—it, my suit, and my car were now crumpled.

Dejected, I called work and went home. The rest of the afternoon slowly passed before everything sank in. I played that morning over and over in my head. Coincidence? Dumb luck? I didn't know what to call it. Later that evening, a friend recommended that I call it "simply a blessing."

A few days passed before I let Jake back into my life. I fought hard to move on without his presence. I tried to apply some semblance of logic to our relationship by thinking he was just an imaginary friend, or maybe he was just wishful thinking, or maybe he was me, a smarter me that I could never give myself credit for. All of those possibilities, however, were shattered by the numerous "coincidences" that seemed to follow on the heels of every other word Jake uttered. From the car accident, to strange encounters with people who would shape and mold my spiritual life, to unerringly accurate dreams and predictions, Jake had proven that he was the real thing.

At this point one might think that Jake had been sent to wear me down and prepare me for my future connection to the archangels. Well, that would be a safe assumption. The angels, however, would get no warmer a reception from me than Jake did. In fact, I held their feet even closer to the fire because of the sheer power their presence exuded. Even though Jake was my spirit guide, his energies still felt very human to me. The angels, on the other hand, possessed a power that I was wholly unfamiliar with.

Though I was raised with a solid Christian foundation, I wasn't really taught to believe in angels. I viewed them merely as biblical figures that had gone the way of miracles like the parting of the Red Sea and turning water into wine— they no longer existed.

Now as I look back at my youth, I wonder how it was so easy for me to dismiss God's messengers when my entire childhood had been riddled with paranormal encounters. I had regularly spotted and interacted with the ghosts in my *very* haunted house. Accurate premonitions were common for me. But into my teens, all the paranormal activity seemed to stop despite my yearning to experiment with it.

As a child, it had all frightened me. As a teenager, I found it intriguing. As a young adult, I simply thought myself crazy and unwilling to let go of an overactive imagination. The world of the paranormal was now affecting my life in a way that I truly wanted no part of. After all, I was burdened enough with my parents telling me what to do and how to live; I sure as hell didn't want ghosts, angels, or anything else yelling at me.

No, the last thing I wanted was for even more authoritative figures to try to control what I did or how I perceived the world. Jake had appeared in my life on the heels of my leaving the church after having become a born-again Christian. I had been raised mostly Lutheran with a sprinkling of Pentecostal whenever my mom got bored of singing tired hymns at our Lutheran church. When she was in the mood for a foot-stomping, Bible-thumping, Holy Ghost–filled service, she had dragged me to whatever Pentecostal or Baptist church she could find.

My father, however, being more sedate and perhaps a bit more conservative, had avoided the loud, high-octane, fashion-driven services and relegated himself to the silence and serenity of his church of forty years. With my diverse upbringing serving as the foundation for becoming born-again, I can't say that I was ripe for paranormal activity to return to my life. According to Christianity, interacting with such things as ghosts was not only seen as taboo, but was considered something that could very well jeopardize one's salvation. Ghosts and things such as spirit guides were considered harbingers of evil, messengers of Satan. And depending on whom you spoke to, angels fell into that category as well, since the belief was that one need only speak to Jesus and God.

My real-life experiences would seriously challenge those beliefs. I struggled and warred with them, so much so that it nearly led me to suicide ... *twice*. I was so tormented and confused that I wanted to throw everything out of my life, leave college, and become a Catholic nun. I thought that if I could sequester myself in a sacred place of worship and live every waking hour on holy ground, then the ghosts, premonitions, and everything else considered unholy would stop.

Bouncing between belief and non-belief—with the discovery of non-Christian religions, the guilt of pondering their validity, and my desire to learn more about them—was a vicious cycle of psychological and emotional anguish that I wouldn't wish on my worst enemy ... if I had one. After hours of kneeling in tear-soaked prayer and begging for God to make sense of the insanity that was my spiritual life, I slowly came to the realization that Jake wasn't an agent of evil, nor were the angels. Years of fighting against my belief in them ceased when I took on Archangel Gabriel—the angel of the Annunciation himself—and lost.

A Growing Acceptance

Jake had seen me through the death of my father and then my mother four years later. I wasn't even thirty and here I was alone in the world. Completely alone. As the only child of parents who had no close ties to their own siblings and distant relatives, I had no family to turn to when they left me.

Blessedly, in my continued quest for spiritual understanding—a quest that had been an obsession of mine from the cradle—I found family I didn't know I had.

One Saturday afternoon, I was sitting in a local diner trying to finish a screenwriting project for film school. Thanks to Jake, I had acquired a near-obsessive passion for the craft, but I was exhausted. The diner was open twenty-four hours a day, and I had been there all night and all morning, which wasn't unusual for me. The lunch crowd was starting to fill the tables. With Mom and Dad gone, the family home seemed cold and unwelcoming, not to mention the last things I wanted to talk to were the resident ghosts that had haunted the house since we moved in when I was four.

For months since I had begun film school while juggling a full-time, overbearing corporate job, the diner had become my home. I was subsisting on a mere four hours of sleep a night and eating all the wrong foods. But I really didn't care. Being at the diner surrounded by the chatter of its patrons was infinitely better than sitting at home alone. Besides, I had befriended one of the waitresses there. She was the only staff member who didn't seem to care if I rented one of her tables all night. I'd arrive around nine in the evening and hang out until her shift ended around dawn, if not later. In between running orders, she would come and sit with me, and we'd chat about everything from men to movies to local gossip and everything in between.

That Saturday, however, the long, sleepless nights, overtime at work, the school project, bottomless cups of coffee, and an endless stream of chilidogs had finally taken their toll. My waitress friend approached my table to fill my coffee cup when she stopped suddenly to stare at me.

"Honey, you look like death warmed over," she said in a charming, Southern drawl.

"I know," I groaned as I drew my hands over my face. "I seriously need to get some rest, but I can't sleep. It seems as if no matter how tired I am, I can't sleep for more than an hour or so at a time." I truly felt as if I were standing on the threshold of death, and judging by my friend's strained features, I must have looked that way, too.

"You need Native American dream tea," she said as she stood there with the pot of coffee in one hand and her other hand on her hip. Curious, my brow arched as I discreetly looked around to see if there were any patrons within earshot.

"Is it legal?" I whispered. I'd never taken Tylenol, much less experimented with any illegal drugs. Paralyzing fear of my parents if they should ever catch me engaging in anything illicit had kept me on the straight and narrow.

My friend's eyes twinkled with mirth as she chuckled, "Yes, sweetie, it's very legal. You can get it at a tea shop up north. It's about forty minutes away in Canterbury Village, but worth the trip."

"Ugh," I said, instantly turned off. I hated shopping, but more than that, I hated touristy places. And with the way I was feeling, I knew I would have little tolerance for driving forty minutes to a place for some novelty tea that may or may not work. "No thanks," I said as I sipped on my coffee.

"Don't be so quick to shoot it down, Chantel. I think you'd like this place. It's owned by an intuitive healer."

Now *that* got my attention. My bleary eyes shot up again to gaze at the waitress.

"She's a real sweetheart," she continued. "And just by looking at you, gal, I think you could use a session or . . . three with her. You should go." With that, she left me to tend to her other customers. I remained quietly sitting at the table, wondering if the trip would be worth it. *Intuitive healer, huh?*

Nah. I shook my head and quickly dismissed the prospect of going.

Later that night, I met another friend for dinner. She was bubbly that evening. Well, bubblier than normal. I could tell from the moment we met in the parking lot that something good had happened to her that day, and as weary as I felt, I was eager to hear some good news.

"Oh my God, Chantel. I had the most awesome day today!" She bounced in her seat as we munched on an appetizer. "I think I found the perfect place to have my wedding... well, if I ever get married."

I chuckled at her exuberance. Both of us were single. And while I was quite content to be boyfriendless, she was ever searching for a man and dreaming of a ridiculously extravagant wedding. I sat and listened as she rattled off every detail of the place she had visited only hours earlier—around the same time I had been sitting at the diner talking with my waitress friend.

After letting her describe every minute detail, I finally interrupted her. "Well, where is this place?"

"Oh, Chantel, you gotta go with me to see it. It's up at Canterbury Village!"

I dropped my fork onto my plate. I could have easily dismissed this as a coincidence, but neither of my friends knew each other. They didn't even know *of* each other. And to have them both mention a place I had never before heard of was just too bizarre.

Needless to say, a few weeks later, I found myself driving forty minutes north to visit the tourist attraction. Though

I'm sure the restaurants and Christmas store were pleasant sites to visit, I had only one place in mind—the tea shop.

Hesitantly, I entered the quaint little store. Tranquil and homey, it was packed wall to wall with merchandise. From tea cups and accessories to books and jewelry, the store seemed to offer an eclectic line of products for tea connoisseurs as well as spiritual seekers. After making a few rounds of the store, I finally gathered up enough nerve to inquire about the intuitive healer my waitress friend had told me about.

"Um, I'm here to see the healer," I said as I slowly approached the lady behind the counter. Behind her was a wall of jars, all containing various blends of teas from around the world. (By God, I didn't know that many different flavors existed!)

"To see whom?" the lady said, peering at me from over the rims of her glasses. She looked at me as if I were an alien. It was then that I thought perhaps I was in the wrong shop.

"The healer? I was told that there was a spiritual healer who worked here," I elaborated.

"That would be me," said a voice from over my shoulder. When I turned to gaze into the warmest and wisest eyes I'd ever seen, I was rendered speechless. For a moment, we stood there in silence as something strange passed between us. To this day, I struggle to pinpoint exactly what that was, but it was accompanied by feelings of familiarity, comfort, joy, and peace.

The woman placed her hands on my shoulders as I stood there dumbfounded. "I'm Ella. It's about time you came home. I've been waiting for you," she said as she hugged me, and instantly my tears began to flow. I wrapped my arms around her tightly, and in that moment all the pain and confusion I had been wrought with since my mother passed months earlier disappeared. I somehow had found my way home to a family I didn't even know I had.

Upon our very first meeting, Ella and I had a connection and bond that would have taken most people years to develop. I felt as if I had known her my whole life, and as she kicked into spiritual mentor mode, I found myself eager to learn whatever she was willing to teach me. Whether it was about tea, tea culture, or my intuitive gifts, she was never lacking in wisdom. I willingly walked along the path she carefully laid out before me, a path that would ultimately lead to one of my greatest moments of spiritual growth. She became my adopted mother, and it was through her tender nurturing and encouragement that I finally came to understand and accept my intuitive gifts.

Through meditation and honing my skills, I learned to connect with the Realm of Spirit in ways I never thought possible. I grew more accepting not only of Gabriel's presence in my life, but of all of divinity. From listening intently to Jesus's instruction, to visiting a cloud temple occupied by the Hindu gods Shiva, Kali, and Ganesh, to seeking out the wisdom and compassion of Kwan Yin, I finally arrived at the conclusion that there was so much more to the Realm of Spirit than religious texts even touched upon.

With my eyes wide open and my curiosity more ravenous than ever, I pondered why religions clawed at each other's throats and vied for followers and their undying loyalty. Why had history been riddled with wars and conflicts, all brought about by one group claiming their god was the bigger god, when in the Realm of Spirit, I could meditate peacefully in my mountain retreat which Jesus and Mary Magdalene, hand in hand, often visited. I could then turn around and visit Archangel Uriel's fiery mansion to play fetch with his two pet dragons only to later speak with the Council—a cluster of twelve entities that offer wisdom and issue decrees for humans as well as the archangels. All the years of being taught that one religious belief was the only way to some promised salvation just couldn't stand up to real, tangible experience with the divine itself.

Through my spiritual travels and under the instruction of Ella and Archangel Gabriel, I finally arrived at the understanding that we all come from one Source. All of us. I believe that every single creature and entity in this universe is crafted by the hands of the same Creator, a being that I still have trouble comprehending, but one that I still refer to as God. We are all his children, and it is to him that we are to return.

One might think that my acceptance of my intuitive gifts and my interactions with the Realm of Spirit would cause me to abandon the religious teachings I grew up with. Not entirely. I didn't have to leave my Christian faith to become accepting of the faiths of others. Though I embrace and respect the philosophies of many religions and those who follow them, the cornerstone of my life remains Jesus of Nazareth. He is my mentor, but more than that, he is my family. He is my father, and to him I am answerable for everything I do in this lifetime.

Though I embrace this pantheism with great conviction, it was not a belief that I was able to adopt overnight. Even now, there are days when years of religious conditioning rear their ugly head and whisper in the back of my mind, *What if you're wrong?* I've had my surlier moments when I've pretended that I couldn't hear Jesus or the angels calling me to offer their instruction or to discuss some aspect of my life. Doing so has often led to a life crisis that forced me to turn my attention in their direction. I know that if I'm wrong, they will tell me and then body-slam me onto the proper path—repeatedly, if need be, until I am sore, winded, and making a timeout gesture with my hands.

"All right, I surrender. You win," I've often said after being set aright by the powers that be. And that's just after arguing with them over the next book or taking on a new client!

As I've walked this life's path, I've grown savvy to the angels' spiritual wrestling techniques. As I mentioned earlier, I wanted nothing to do with "God's plan." Gabriel called acceptance of my destiny a walk of faith; I called it unemployment. Either way, I lost the battle. In fact, I nearly lost my life, but there are days when I scoff and say death may have been the easier path. After losing everything I owned, including irreplaceable treasures such as my childhood photos and family heirlooms with more sentimental than monetary value, I sometimes wonder why I even bother getting up every morning. But then I'll get e-mails such as this:

Dear Chantel,

I just wanted to thank you for writing your books and being brave enough to talk about the angels and discuss the real problems many of us face when it comes to spirituality. Like you, I've encountered many a dark day and questioned my belief in God, but then I stop and look at my life through the angels' eyes and realize that everything has a purpose—not just my life, but all the good and bad that comes with it. Thank you for helping me to make peace with myself and showing me how to focus more on how to endure and learn from every lesson God brings before me.

So many times I have received letters asking for prayers and intercessions for people in some of the most harrowing circumstances imaginable. I find myself so badly wanting to write back and say that all will be well, that it will all work out in the end. But the truth is, it might work out, but it might not. When I look up into the eyes of an archangel, seeking an answer either way, he may answer me or he may simply fold his arms, shake his head, and deny my request for insight—or, in many cases, foresight.

For some whom I've read for, the angels have offered up a few predictions, though not many. I'm not in the business of making predictions, and neither are the angels, for that matter. Like them, my life's purpose is to simply guide and offer wisdom. But unlike them, I cannot see the future, not even my own, and I've lost count of the days where it's galled me that I can sit and talk with the legendary Archangel Michael and not even get a winning lottery number while my phone is ringing off the hook with calls from bill collectors.

All in all, working with the angels, or divinity as a whole, does not make life easier by any stretch of the imagination. There are days when I think what many see as a gift of intuition is really more a burden. The responsibility that comes with it is oppressive, to say the least. Any medium with a genuine connection to the divine, and with even a modicum of self-respect, knows that it's not a matter to be taken lightly, because in the end, we are answerable to a Higher Power, the very one that sends the archangels to connect with us to begin with.

Ironically, the mighty sting of being in direct employment of the divine is not too dissimilar to being in the service of humans. It's your job to keep your employer happy and pleased with your work, but you can't really expect your employer to reciprocate that favor. In fact, Michael has told me on more than one occasion, "It's not our job to make you happy." And he's right. The archangels' vows are many, but making us humans happy ain't one of them. Invariably, that is our job, and based on my many years of working with clients and even looking back at my own life, I have to say that we humans generally suck at creating real, lasting happiness. I liken it to sand. We can pick up happiness here and there by the fistful, but for whatever reason, it tends to slip through our fingers, leaving only a few grains ... remnants of what once was. And then, like the foolish humans we are, we pick up another handful.

All the while, the archangels watch over us. Most look on with compassion in their eyes. Others cant their heads in bemusement of just how dense the human race is. Still others roll their eyes or turn away with a scowl of disdain. Regardless of an angels' feelings toward us, they all express the same sentiment: "And to think you humans asked to come here."

Yep, that's the crux of it. We asked for this, and now that we're here, we're searching for something, anything, to fill us with the same feeling of elation that can only be gotten in the spirit world anyhow! Archangel Uriel says we're slow learners, while Archangel Michael takes a more diplomatic approach and says we're simply brave, adventurous souls.

Whatever we are, we're here under the watchful eyes of the archangels, our brothers and sisters in spirit, the ones entrusted to guide us and bring about our fate, however it must come. They're a hodgepodge of personalities that I find entertaining most of the time and frustrating at others. As an angel medium, I wish my life could be like a Hollywood movie where I get to go on cool adventures and play the heroine that gets the guy in the end, but such is not the case.

No, I get to live my life just as normally as anyone else, with perhaps a more acute sense of awareness of the goings-on in the spiritual world. Most of the time I tend to tune it all out, but when it comes knocking and I'm given an assignment from the Throne, I have to rise to the occasion. As with any job, there are good days and bad days. There are days when I say I could never live without the archangels by my side, and there are days when I wish I had never met an archangel. Either way, I recognize that working with them is an invaluable life experience, one that will no doubt affect me long after I'm done with this world.

I would never discourage anyone from pursuing such connections to the Heavenly Hosts. Even if the angels don't give you the answers you seek, you can at the very least be comforted by the fact that they are there. If there is a bonus to being a medium, it's not having an easier life or having all the answers to the toughest life challenges, but knowing that there is someone on your team rooting for you. There is someone you can trust and know will love you unconditionally. There is someone who finds no fault in you even if you find it in yourself. There is someone who will carry you when you can't walk another step.

The archangels, your spiritual siblings, will never leave your side. By divine law, they are bound to us, as all have taken vows to fulfill their divine purpose, which includes helping us humans fulfill ours.

chapter two

ANGELS ALL AROUND US

Everyone has the ability to connect with their angels on some level. I believe that every human was bestowed with the gift of intuition, a gift that comes in myriad shapes, colors, and sizes. The extent of one's intuition varies as greatly as the people in the world, and I'm certain that no two gifts are exactly alike, mostly due to the understanding that intuition is a purely subjective mechanism. Whispers from the divine are filtered through our own human thoughts, emotions, and desires, and because of this, I feel it will be a very long time before the skill can be measured by science. There are just too many variables to take into account.

Still, I know from nearly twenty years of experience that intuition is very real and very powerful; and if honed properly, it can help you to build an intimately close and lasting relationship with the archangels—the angels to whom Heaven delegated the task of working directly with humans.

No doubt you've seen many a book that covers the topic of angel communication. You may have even stumbled across my previous works, *Azrael Loves Chocolate, Michael's A Jock* and *The Angel Code*. Both books present angels in a practical, tangible way that makes it easier for us to accept our gift of intuition and to better understand and get to know the angels. Doing so can help us to initiate and facilitate a deeper, more meaningful connection with the divine.

But my purpose doesn't stop there.

As you read previously, a close relationship with the angels can be very much like a close relationship with family. Most days you love them and welcome their presence, but other days you just want to be alone. Regardless, I feel that establishing a conscious connection with the divine can yield invaluable insight and wisdom. For as obstinate as I've been and for as flustered as I've been with life circumstances in the past, there is one thing I can never deny: the angels have always brought to my attention the reasons that I had to endure such difficult challenges. *Always.* Without them and their commitment to remain by my side, I would not have made it this far. So I can say with complete conviction that we as humans should seek to establish and foster a relationship with our cosmic siblings. While I don't believe it will make your life easier by any means, it will make life easier to grasp. Also, you will cease to merely exist and go through day-to-day routines, and will begin to live and see purpose and meaning in everything you do and everything around you.

Better still, it can lead to an increased awareness and understanding of yourself. Engaging the archangels helps one's eyes to open to the realities, as well as the illusions, we humans tussle with every day. And when you seek out the divine wisdom of these celestial hosts, it helps you to better understand the whys and hows that vex us in daily life.

When getting to know the angels, you want to go beyond what you may have read in typical "how to talk to an angel" books. This is not about simply invoking or summoning the angels to help us in a crisis. We're looking to nurture a much deeper, more personal connection where we will truly be able to recognize the angels as something more than intangible creatures that fly among us unseen. We want to be able to recognize them for what they truly are—our siblings, our family in spirit, who are here to help guide us through each and every experience we encounter, no matter how stubborn we may be and no matter how unhappy we may be with the spiritual path we're currently on.

About the Archangels

When I use the term *angel*, I am often referring to Heaven's archangels. The archangels are some of the most beautiful and awe-inspiring creatures that humans will ever lay eyes upon. These angels have been with us since the birth of humanity and have been weaving throughout growing civilizations and countless cultures since before the written word. Once humans began pondering their place in the cosmos, they began to look up to the skies and within themselves for the answers. Once people began asking the big questions of *Who am I?* and *Why am I here?*, the archangels began to make their presence known as ambassadors of the Source. They became the voice, and at times even the physical presence, through which the unfathomable power of the Source would manifest.

Today, angels seem to have been relegated strictly to the New Age and religion sections of bookstores, but I can't be emphatic enough when I say that there is absolutely nothing New Age about the Hosts of Heaven. They have been with us since the dawn of time, long before any organized religion was ever established. And while the angels are indeed divine creatures, they are not *religious* beings. Of course, they are recognized today in the sister religions of Judaism, Christianity, and Islam—as well as other religions, if you look hard enough—but the angels themselves have never subscribed to any one religion. They are here for all of us, regardless of our religious beliefs or even lack thereof.

The word *angel* literally means "messenger," and the archangels—or chief messengers—are the many different manifestations of the Source that serve as communication channels between the Source and our reality. They are the conductors of the cosmos who walk with humanity to help carry out what Archangel Michael calls "God's Great Equation."

In sum, they are the divine custodians of fate.

As you read previously and will read later on in this book, building a relationship with the angels was no easy task for me initially. I'm writing this book and laying out all my faults to help you avoid the many pitfalls I've encountered. Not only do I want to supply you with useful, accurate information on the angels so you can better get to know them, but I also want to help you better understand them and their personalities. Yes, just like us humans, angels have personalities.

Since my previous two books were released, I've received countless e-mails and have been asked in interviews why these divine messengers feel they have to display human traits such as a preference for a certain color, food, or kind of music.

These sound like things we might see on a social networking page—actually it was a social networking page that prompted me to begin asking the angels such questions. While an angel's love for spicy Mexican food may seem trite or even absurd, I can assure you it is not.

The angels show us their "human" side so we can better relate to them. It also helps immensely with connecting and communicating with the angels because, although humans possess intuitive skills, we all utilize those skills differently. So knowing that Archangel Cassiel has a love for industrial music whereas Haniel's heart thumps to the rhythm of bluegrass can help when discerning their signs and messages.

This also means that we'll resonate better with some angels than others. I must admit that my growing relationship with Archangel Gabriel was incredibly rocky in the beginning. The angel's meticulous and militant nature proved to be an irritant for me on many an occasion because I completely lacked the discipline that he demands. The interesting part is that irritation often motivates and moves me into action. So while it's uncomfortable for me to work with Gabriel from time to time, at least things get done. And that's all that matters.

I resonate best with Archangel Cassiel. As I recounted in *The Angel Code*, he's the only archangel I've seen with my physical eyes. I'm not sure if I feel closer to him because he's the first archangel I formally met or because we both share a love for Goth fashion and horror movies, but his quiet, gentle, and hands-off nature when it comes to guiding my life is something I not only appreciate, but welcome. Whenever Cassiel is around, I feel secure and inspired. Whenever Gabriel is around, however, I tend to be grumpy—and he couldn't care less. Like a strict parent, he doesn't care if I sulk while cleaning my room, so long as I clean it.

You, too, will find that you communicate better with certain angels. Perhaps you and your favorite angel share a love of certain foods or cultures, or perhaps the angel's presence brings you a greater sense of peace. Not everyone will find Raziel's abrasiveness and brutal honesty comforting. Some will, however. Likewise, not everyone will find solace in Sandalphon's ability to be the most adorable poster angel for a greeting-card shop. We all have different tastes, and there will always be an angel we can best connect with.

Beginning the Human Experience ... with the Archangels

When I took a peek into Archangel Raguel's position as Heaven's ultimate taskmaster, I witnessed an angel renowned for two things: speed and efficiency. Raguel's list of duties is long and far-reaching, but where we humans are concerned, he's charged with helping us begin our journey from the Realm of Spirit into whichever human reality we wish to participate in. Additionally, he is a messenger of messengers, since he also notifies other archangels of new tasks, duties, or assignments. And considering that there are more archangels than we can count, speed and efficiency are paramount. In fact, Archangel Michael has expressed that Raguel moves so fast among them that not even the angels can see or detect his presence.

One might wonder that with the limitless powers darting around Heaven and with the limitless power of the very Source itself why there would even be a need for a taskmaster angel such as Raguel. After all, cannot the angels simply communicate among themselves with abilities that we humans might liken to telepathy? The answer to that is simple, and it's an answer that is most times Michael's go-to when I ask him questions about the power of the Heavenly Hosts and how efficient such powers could make life for every sentient being in existence: *Just because you can doesn't mean you should.*

Everything in our universe was created for a purpose. Raguel's purpose is to help keep angelic tasks running smoothly. Whether there is an actual need for him is irrelevant. The point is the Source created him for such a job, and Raguel does it with flawless dedication. My personal theory is that Raguel is another way for the Source to provide a visual for human souls to learn from while engaged in the human experience.

My spirit guide Jake recounted, "One moment I can be standing, just chatting with other angels, and the next I'm standing there with a new assignment in my hand. Before I can even say thank you, Raguel has most likely already crossed off two dozen other stops from his list. He's just that fast." Speedy or otherwise, the archangel has his personal thoughts on humans rotating in and out of different realities, like Disney World patrons running from one ride to another.

"I don't get it. And I'm grateful that it's not my job *to* get it," the angel groaned as he rubbed his temples. I then asked him how he felt about running requests back and forth for the countless human souls so ready and eager to experience … life.

"It's almost as if human souls can't exist in peace and harmony for any great length of time. They're like children who can't sit still!" In the years I've gotten to know Raguel,

I consider him one of the curtest and most brutally honest archangels I've ever met. One might even consider him a bit cold at times, as he's not the most social of butterflies, yet when posed with questions regarding humanity, he has no problem displaying his annoyance and exasperation.

"Humans leave the peace and perfection that is Heaven only to find themselves seeking that same peace and perfection in a reality they know has everything but," Raguel grumbled before fading from the sight of my intuitive eye. I didn't expect to get much out of the archangel on the inner workings of how and why we humans come to be in this world, so I knew I'd have to talk to a few other angels to gain a bit more insight.

For the most part, when someone decides to venture into a human reality, Raguel's the man...or angel...to see. After getting the Source's approval of the spiritual field trip, we're then assigned a chaperone, or parent angel—the angel that will remain with us from the moment we're born until we return home. Initially, I wasn't sure who to talk to about that part of the process, but to my surprise and sheer joy, Metatron volunteered.

If I could describe Archangel Metatron in one word, it would be "fatherly." This sweet and soft-spoken angel has a powerful presence. Also known as "Little YHWH," he's the tallest angel in Heaven; and as Michael puts it, you don't argue with someone whose height is measured in light years.

Keeping that in mind, humility comes easy when talking with this angel. All the snarkiness that I tend to express when conversing with the other archangels flies right out the window whenever Metatron is near. Even though he's the second youngest angel in Heaven, having only been created after Earth first came to be, he seems to have retained his elderly vibrations from when he was the biblical prophet Enoch. That's the only ancient attribute about this angel.

Though some of my clients have seen Metatron in human form, I have yet to. When the archangel appears to me, he does so as a white mist with hints of shimmering rainbow colors or as a large, billowing cloud in the shape of a hand. When he's near, I can't deny the sense of peace that flows over me. Even if I've had a bad day or a heated exchange with another angel, Metatron always seems to soothe me, and so I sat eagerly awaiting what the gentle angel would have to say about human souls and the process they go through before they're born.

"Well, I agree with Raguel in that humans are childlike and don't particularly enjoy sitting in one place for any great length of time. The Source, or God as many call it, in infinite wisdom knows this and that's why your world, and many others, exist," the angel said with a bit of amusement in his voice.

Many Others?

A few years ago, I encountered a client whose past life seemed to have occurred in the *future*. His space-age existence looked like something pulled out of the recesses of Gene Roddenberry's mind, and the vision left me not only stammering through the consultation, but also screaming at the angels, begging for an explanation of how I was seeing the future in the past. This is when they explained to me that this universe is vast, with many realities existing simultaneously. In addition to selecting the reality we wish to experience, we also must select the time-line in which we wish to experience it.

In essence, your past life does not necessarily have to be in the past, or even on the same timeline, of the current reality in which you're living. In the Realm of Spirit, souls may choose whatever life they wish, whether it takes place in ancient Rome, feudal Japan, a United States in the very distant "future" of this reality, or even an entirely different world altogether.

Metatron expressed that the human soul is by nature a curious and transient creature; and its unrelenting curiosity, fueled by the desire to experience every aspect of human "life," is what carries a soul from one adventure to another.

The answer as to why souls engage in the human experience is simple: because they can.

But I think what's most important here is that the Source also encourages us to explore.

"For as long as the human spirit wishes to engage in these experiences, our collective spiritual consciousness will continue to create worlds for them," Metatron revealed.

Now that little tidbit of information shocked me. "So God is still creating worlds for souls to see and visit?"

"Of course," Metatron chuckled. "It's not like we'll ever run out of space."

And to think poor Metatron is the one in charge of maintaining the Akashic Records, a massive, immeasurable library wherein every life and event in this universe is recorded. Talk about job security! I don't think he has to worry about losing his any time soon.

So here we humans are, adventurous children of the Source, a higher power that seems to enjoy spoiling us by creating any reality that will keep us busy and entertained on into eternity. All one needs to do is to have the desire to go exploring, send a request in Raguel's direction, and then get assigned an archangel that will assist in hammering out the details of one's experience. Liken Raguel to a travel agent.

And here is where I step into hot water every time. I've expressed this in my previous books, consultations, and lectures, and I have to say that of all the ideas and philosophies I've explored, this one revelation has been met with the most opposition. It seems that people are very willing to believe in God, gods, ascended masters, and angels, but the moment I tell everyone that we are coauthors of the lives we're living, that everything you and I are experiencing was already written and approved by us, is the moment I wind up with pitchfork-wielding hordes ready to burn me at the stake.

Okay, it's not that bad, but it's pretty darn close. From a radio-show host angrily expressing that there was no way in hell he could have written, much less approved, his less-than-stellar life, to frustrated e-mails and even more angst-laden book reviews, I have faced the same amount of ire that I basically dished out to Archangel Gabriel when he first gave me the revelation. And I wasn't even as eloquent as the people confronting me. When Gabriel said that the misery in my life was of my own doing, I came back with one simple word: "Bullshit."

But not only did the angel show me the very moment that I consulted him about the current life I'm living, he also showed me the moment when he actually tried to *stop me*. Talk about adding insult to injury!

The reason we script these dramatic lives that are worthy of pay-per-view is because we know that none of it is real. Sure, if I stub my toe on the edge of the bed, it sure as hell will feel real. My anger and frustration over my illness and everything that ensued felt real. The depression from solitude and constant struggle with thoughts of suicide were painfully real. Still, in the end, it's all merely a learning experience. It's our thirst to discover more about ourselves—and God's willingness to allow us to go through it—that keeps us forever returning to these existences.

When Gabriel gave me the vision of the two of us sitting on a lawn discussing what is now my current life's script, I didn't want to believe it. I wanted to think that if I truly had a say in how my life went, I would create one of supreme happiness and comfort. You know, something pretty darn close to Heaven, which then of course begs the question of why I even bothered leaving Heaven to begin with.

"I'm not coming this way again. It's too difficult," I grumbled as I shook my head incredulously.

"You said that last time," Gabriel quipped.

And here, years after that revelation, I catch myself daydreaming about my next lifetime. Oh yeah, I've got it all planned out, right down to the painful lessons I'll need to learn as a child to forge me into the adult I want to be. Sometimes I'll catch and berate myself for plotting out my next life as if I were writing a book of fiction. Then I'll sit and wonder if I included the challenges because my higher self recognizes that they serve as valuable life lessons that help to forge one's personality. Or maybe I'm just a sick, sadistic old biddy. A lot of days I opt for the latter, but in the end one thing is for certain: the Source would never allow us to write anything into our scripts that we couldn't handle. No matter what, we must always remember that we are only here for two reasons: because we want to be and because the Source allows us to be. So if your soul is incapable of dealing with the fast-paced, controversial life of Jim Morrison, forget about coming back as the iconic rock star.

I bet you didn't see that coming.

A few years ago, the surviving members of the Doors were guests on the popular paranormal radio show *Coast to Coast AM*. As the discussion progressed, the members began relating stories of how so many kids today are still vying to stand in the spot that was once held by Jim Morrison. One of the members scoffed that too often guys would say to him that they were Morrison reincarnated. The general sentiment was, "You and everyone else I talk to, kid." After that comment, I turned off the radio. He was scoffing at a notion that was very much close to the truth.

One of the reasons the general public mocks and ridicules people who claim they were Cleopatra or Christopher Columbus in a past life is because so many people make the same claim. After all, there can only be one Joan of Arc and only one Genghis Khan, right? Wrong. If you have the spiritual fortitude and constitution to endure the life you chose, have fun. Just remember that whatever "notable" life you choose is already plotted out. If you really want to experience what it's like to be the Lizard King, then you'll have to take all the bad with the good. Could you alter a few aspects? Sure, why not? But the point is to experience that life as it originally happened.

After all, this reality only knows one Jim Morrison, as it were. I would be foolish not to entertain the notion that there are other realities with other, perhaps happier outcomes for his life. The possibilities are infinite and the only limitation is you. Much like levels in a video game, you can only unlock or engage an existing life script once you've achieved a certain degree of mastery. And to do that takes experience and practice.

For the record, no human has gained enough mastery to return as Jesus. As of the writing of this book, he's still holding the high score for that life experience. Same goes for Buddha. There are quite a few figures we are familiar with that haven't had repeat performances, either because no one is proficient enough or because no one desires to experience that life script. Judas and Hitler are two lives that humans tend to avoid for obvious reasons. When we return home to the Realm of Spirit, we bring with us the memories and feelings of the life we just lived, and no one wants to carry in their soul such harrowing experiences. For a better understanding of how this works, please read Gabriel's recounting of Jesus's story in appendix B.

In fact, those two scripts of Judas and Hitler, to name a few, were never meant to be carried out by human souls anyhow. Much of the darkness we see in this world in particular isn't driven by humans. Instead, such tasks are delegated to other entities created specifically for that purpose. I'll venture more into that later. Until then, there's a lot more ground to cover. After all, you're just standing here with a script and a parent angel who has made a vow to watch over you for however long you've chosen to live.

So while your mother is uttering foul curses at your dad, who's trying to document your birth with his video camera, what exactly is going on with you—aside from all the physiological chaos that you've just been thrown into? Well, based on the opinion of clients and those I've spoken to in passing regarding the subject of human souls, the majority seem to believe that our souls descend from Heaven or are created either at the time of conception or at the time of birth.

Well, the angels have already shown us that our souls are alive and well long before we decide to venture into the human experience. What I found surprising, however, is that our souls don't really *descend* from anywhere. All my life, I was of the thought that we "come down" from Heaven to live on Earth. But I now understand that to be a very archaic way of thinking.

In our universe, there is no up or down, no here or there, no past or future. Everything takes place on the same plane, just at different vibrations or frequencies. In fact, the use of terms such as "the other side" or "Realm of Spirit" is just a way of expressing what our human minds have difficulty grasping. People tend to think of God, the angels, and human souls as "over there" or "up there" because they can't see them, hear them, or touch them.

But according to what Archangel Gabriel revealed to me, we are all coexisting in the same space at the same time. The reason we humans can't see the spiritual world is much the same reason we can't see the flickering of an incandescent light bulb. We simply don't possess the ability to detect things that operate at much higher frequencies than we do.

Go ahead, look at that forty-watt bulb in your desk lamp. It doesn't appear to be flickering, does it? But if you were to film the light bulb in slow motion, you would see that its light is indeed pulsing. This is due to the bulb being powered by an alternating current (AC). And the hertz, or what is considered a unit of frequency defined as the number of cycles per second, is moving so rapidly that the human eye is unable to detect it. It is the same for the spirit world; humans are generally unable to detect it because it exists at a much higher frequency than we do.

I have often likened intuition to hyper awareness of the environment in which one lives. But we humans can only go so far. The reason that highly intuitive people can connect with beings on the other side is because those beings lower their frequencies to make communication possible. I was once on a radio show where a "seasoned" psychic claimed that it was difficult for angels to lower their frequencies to connect with humans. I just shook my head and sighed. The angels aren't the ones who are limited, *we are*.

And we're fully aware of such limitations when we decide to live in this reality.

So, if we don't descend from Heaven and we don't walk through some proverbial tunnel, how do we get here? Well, how do you enter your dreams at night? You put your head on a pillow, cuddle up in your blanket, and go to sleep.

And that's how we come to be here. What we have considered to be the human soul is actually our human consciousness. Our soul is very safe and comfortable at home in Heaven. What is engaged in the human experience is our avatar. Now, this concept was explored long before James Cameron's movie of the same name or films like *The Matrix*.

The word avatar is derived from Sanskrit's *avatārah,* which literally means "descent." It comes from *avatarati: ava,* meaning "away," plus *tarati,* which means "he crosses over."

The word avatar is often used in Hinduism to illustrate a god's manifestation in the human world. But in the computer age, it has come to describe "an electronic image that represents and is manipulated by a computer user (as in a computer game)," according to the dictionary. Gods, human souls, or your level eighty-five Blood Elf mage in *World of Warcraft* ... it's all relative.

When Gabriel first explained this to me, I became giddy and started to imagine that I was somewhere in a pod and connected to some large computer, like Neo in *The Matrix*. What the angel showed me, however, blew that notion out of the water.

"Look up," the archangel instructed during one of my visitations to the Realm of Spirit through meditation. "What do you see?"

"The stars," I said, gazing up into the darkness of space. But I knew there was something very different about the sky in the Realm of Spirit from the sky I was so used to gazing at in my waking hours. Unlike in the human world, the stars weren't sparse against a sea of black. Instead, there were many clustered together in a grid-like formation.

Gabriel took my hand and led me upward to get a closer look. The closer we came to the grid, the more I realized what I was seeing: human souls, countless human souls. They were all orbs of various colors—white, blue, purple, green, gold—and they were all connected by what looked like a colorful stream of plasma. It seemed that this grid went on into eternity.

"Everyone is sleeping," the angel whispered. What was more beautiful than the sight I beheld were all the angels weaving between the souls. Some angels were leading souls to the place where they would be resting during their stay in the human world. Other angels were escorting souls (that had just awoken from their experience) out of the grid and back to the bustling metropolis of Heaven that I had previously visited during another meditation.

And here I ask myself again, *Why did I leave? Why did I leave there to come here?* Uriel says we're slow. Michael says we're brave.

I say we're gluttons for punishment.

So after you connect with your angels, write your script, get it approved, and tuck yourself into bed with your favorite teddy bear. You're ready to embark on the journey of a lifetime—literally.

Good luck.

chapter three

WELCOME TO THE HUMAN EXPERIENCE— ENJOY YOUR STAY!

"You are a walking miracle," Archangel Michael said to me one afternoon as I sat in the confines of a small, dark, and stifling hot room. It was going on a decade, and that one single room had been my hell. My prison. In the beginning, when I took ill, that upstairs room had been a blessing. After all, had it not been for the landlord's willingness to allow me to live there for nothing more than what I offered in gratitude for the shelter, I'd have been on the streets.

There were some days, however, when I wondered if begging on a corner was a bad thing when compared with those circumstances. With a broken body and more progressive illnesses than I could count, walking up and down stairs became more and more difficult. My favorite pastime, cooking, became less of an occurrence because I wasn't able to stand very long in a kitchen. And because it was not my kitchen and rather that of someone who had no respect for the art of cooking or the basic sanitary housekeeping that was necessary with my compromised immune system, I spent more time cleaning it than cooking in it.

After a while, cooking ceased altogether and my meals quickly went from hot but inexpensive and nutritionally empty dinners every night to canned goods that were barely warmed on a sixty-watt light bulb. Depending on the density of the canned food, cooking on a light bulb took hours, and hence, I often ate canned pasta and soups cold. It was just as much of a risk to my health, with the way food is recalled these days, but I could no longer physically clean and cook, nor could I psychologically endure the hell of disdainful gazes or culturally ignorant tirades. Not to mention, being downstairs meant having to listen to consistently loud and grating verbal bashing by those who seemed to think themselves far better than any and everyone who flickered across a television screen. It was the endless, mindless chatter of those who could barely read the newspaper, much less pick up a book.

I went from doing laundry once a month to every six. I went from venturing out of the house with a friend or to write at a café three times a week to once every three months. It seemed that the harder I fought to get back on my feet, the more my health drew me down into misery. It was like treading quicksand, and there was no help in sight.

I could go as long as eight weeks upstairs without a single word from anyone. No one called. No one cared if I lived or not. And during the summers, I sat in the darkness of that room cursing all of humanity. A walking miracle? Me? Sure, if you counted the fact that I have congestive heart failure and asthma and yet somehow survived a room that reached upwards of 103 degrees during the summer. My health and my life were of no consideration to anyone but me, and the more pressing the circumstances became, the less I cared.

I would sit upstairs with a single can of cold beans or ravioli as the scents of baked turkey and ham wafted through the house holiday after holiday, year after year. And as I listened to the hearty cheers and laughter of the merrymakers below, I scoffed at the very archangels who would sit by my side and whisper, "You are loved."

If love came by way of scorn and solitude, then I had it in spades.

"I'm not a walking miracle," I finally clipped in response to Michael's words. "I'm a living, breathing disaster. I'm a statistic waiting to happen." After all, if I had died, the only thing to alert anyone of my passing would have been the stench of my corpse. And though I prayed for death every hour of every day, I dreaded dying with so little dignity. Still, I pondered if it really mattered. Would dignity *really* concern me if I no longer lived on the earth plane among those who knew of me? Knowing my luck, that answer would be yes. Countless days I imagined a hell of being forced to sit in front of some television screen to watch the same world that mocked me in life now mock me in death.

When I looked in the mirror every day, I saw nothing, not a slip of a miracle that Michael spoke of. I only saw raw, unmitigated misery. Still, I held on to the visions that Gabriel had given me, visions of us sitting on a plush, green lawn discussing what this life would be. Every time the archangel pointed to a difficult challenge on the timeline, I would dismissively wave my hand with, "Pshaw, I can handle it."

As I stared at the small confines of my room, those words echoed in my mind and haunted me to the point that I knew I would go insane from it. Yet, here I am. I survived. Despite the burdensome circumstances, I am still here. It is only by God and his messengers that I live and still maintain somewhat of a modicum of dignity. If nothing else in this life, I can hold my head up and say that I have survived a hell that battered me to a bloody pulp.

But it did not … it could not break me. And I'm praying it never does.

Had such a trial come before I had established connections with God's messengers, I would have considered it either a punishment from God or an attack by the Devil. Too often in church during my youth did pastors attribute money problems to the evil machinations of Satan. Too many times had I watched faith healers "heal" by casting out devils that apparently were the cause of an affliction. But now, with clarity and a better understanding of how our reality works, I would be foolish to concur.

Throughout history, religions around the globe have taught humankind of their place in the cosmos. More often than not, adherents have been warned that they have a target on their backs. Their very souls are in the crosshairs as diabolical powers seek to tempt them away from the benevolence of their creator.

Tales of spiritual warfare have followed humanity since the beginning of time, it seems, and have served as explanations for why things happen as they do. If famine strikes a village, then of course a trickster spirit is among them, seeking to torment them. Or worse yet, perhaps the gods of rain and earth have not been appeased. If someone is prosperous, then of course it is only because the person is righteous and has found favor in the eyes of Heaven.

From superstitions passed through oral, cautionary tales to stories of the Bible, such as the book of Job, we are caught up in a never-ending cycle of judgment wherein we take stock of everything in our lives and place them in one of two categories: good or bad.

> 2 And the LORD said unto Satan, From whence comest thou? And Satan answered the LORD, and said, From going to and fro in the earth, and from walking up and down in it. 3 And the LORD said unto Satan, Hast thou considered my servant Job, that there is none like him in the earth, a perfect and an upright man, one that feareth God, and escheweth evil? and still he holdeth fast his integrity, although thou movedst me against him, to destroy him without cause. 4 And Satan answered the LORD, and said, Skin for skin, yea, all that a man hath will he give for his life. 5 But put forth thine hand now, and touch his bone and his flesh, and he will curse thee to thy face. 6 And the LORD said unto Satan, Behold, he is in thine hand; but save his life.

Look out, Job. They're comin' for you, man. They're comin' for you.

So here we have the most righteous man who had ever graced the planet during his days, and Heaven pretty much offered him up on a platter in some sort of unspoken bet. Did I mention he was the most righteous?

When Job was befallen with an acute case of rotten luck, his wife belittled him. His friends, however, heard about it and came from afar to cheer him up. What really stands out here is verse eleven: "Now when Job's three friends heard of all this evil that was come upon him, they came everyone from his own place … to mourn with him and to comfort him." The man had lost his home, his family, his riches, and his health, and it was all attributed to some sort of nefarious plot. Well, the Bible clearly sets the story up for us and shows that it was Satan who did it. Mind you, this was an evil that was permitted by God. God could have easily said no. But he didn't. Without that approval, Job would have continued being righteous and rich until his cushy death.

Unfortunately, such was not to happen.

Stories like this are what keep many of us stuck in the belief that the Devil is after us when bad things occur, or that we must be in God's great favor when good things occur. I believe we have to pull back for a moment and be honest with ourselves. It's time we understood that the notions of good and bad are purely subjective and only describe situations or circumstances that make us uncomfortable to one degree or another. When Job had riches, it was assumed that he was in God's good graces. When he sat upon a pile of ashes, homeless and destitute, everyone around him believed that a great evil was upon him.

These notions of good and bad have been with humankind forever, and I have no doubt that they always will be. Despite the fact that they are subjective and are based purely on one's perspective and how they make one feel, it seems we will never be able to escape their prison of illusion. And for so long as we exist in this reality, we may be hindered from understanding and accepting that life is neither good nor bad, but *simply is*.

What befalls us has nothing to do with devils chasing us or God punishing us, but instead with the lessons we are to learn in this lifetime. If we can train our minds to first examine situations in terms of what we can learn from them instead of wasting energy on blame, we will find our existence far easier to navigate. While the challenges will be no less daunting, the losses no less painful, and the disappointments no less stinging, we will at least find ourselves able to endure much more than we might give ourselves credit for.

Though some of you may be a lot like my old self and therefore hesitant to view spiritual lessons in this light, I still ask you to give this perspective a chance. I believe that actively engaging the divine and connecting directly with our cosmic siblings helps to open our eyes to why we must endure the hardships we do. It helps us to see past the illusions we create in our minds and get to the core of each lesson we must learn. When we see life as *it just is* and are no longer so quick to judge everything as good or bad, there is less room for complacency and a false sense of security when life is good, and less room for panic and worry when life becomes turbulent. Our existence becomes less of a tug of war and more of a string of experiences that we can appreciate for the spiritual growth and maturity they foster.

When you encounter life challenges, try to think of them as a form of spiritual strength training. When you seek to build muscles in your body, you can lift weights, working against gravity, or you can use resistance training. The greater the weight or the resistance, the harder your body has to work and the stronger you become. We can apply the same principles to our spirituality. The adversity, trials, and tribulations we encounter in a lifetime serve as the resistance we need to build our spiritual selves. Without any of these challenges, what could we as spiritual beings hope to learn or achieve?

So how do the archangels fit into all of this? Well, they don't work within the confines of good versus evil, either. They're least concerned with what makes us happy or sad, and more concerned with what serves a divine purpose, God's purpose, your purpose in this reality. They are here to guide us along our chosen script, as well as to create the conditions that motivate us into action—conditions that ultimately bring to us the lessons we're to learn. In essence, the angels are working within the universal law of causality, or cause and effect.

Every action you take creates an effect. Say you leave an upstairs window open while your air conditioning is running. Since the AC will never shut off, your electric bill will be more than you were expecting. Now you will have to pinch pennies for the week when you had already made plans to spend that extra money at the local art fair. So, because you weren't there to purchase a piece of art from a cute, little, freckle-faced kid who was trying to raise money for a new computer, he stayed an extra thirty minutes and instead was discovered by some French philanthropist who took an instant liking to the kid's art.

Of course, that's how it was *supposed* to happen. Still, you're at home watching *I Love Lucy* reruns, cursing the electric company, and bemoaning the fact that you don't have enough cash to go out that weekend. Cause and effect. Like dominoes, everything falls into place. With one action—the tipping of one domino—a string of reactions is set in motion. But unlike dominoes, there's no end to that string. What we initiate in this life will ultimately follow us back home into the Realm of Spirit. That is to say that the decisions we make before come into being as mortals affect our experience and thus impact the decisions we make when we decide to take on the human reality for another round.

With this awareness and understanding of causality, as well as of the Realm of Spirit and our scripted lives, I believe there is no alternative but to acknowledge that we humans are wholly responsible for every experience we have.

Remember what I told Gabriel earlier: *I'm not coming back this way again.* Granted, I said that last time, but this time I mean it … I think.

Regardless of the life we choose, however, the angels will be there creating conditions in our lives to bring about desired effects, which in turn will create a cause in another human's life. There is no such thing as an accident. The dominoes that led up to an incident, as well as the dominoes tipped by that incident, come from and move on into eternity, crossing time and space and affecting every sentient being on one level or another. Liken it to an earthquake in the Far East that in turn creates a tsunami. Across the vast Pacific and across the span of a few hours, that tsunami will be seen creeping toward the shores of California. Such is the way of our decisions and the actions we make in this existence.

Everything we do, from the trivial to the profound, will have an effect not only on our own lives, but on those of others. Whether we call it the Golden Rule, karma, or the butterfly effect, the law of causality is a cosmic wave that sweeps up every single being in existence and carries them through time and into infinity. We cannot escape it, and to acknowledge it is to acknowledge that we are all connected not merely as children of the Source, but we are also connected by the very scripts that we write when we decide to venture into human realms.

Take a minute to consider your life. Look at your past and plot out exactly how you've come to be in this moment. Look at the lives that have affected yours, and vice versa, and how those lives affect other lives, and on and on and on. No, this is not a new concept. There are hundreds if not thousands of books that say this. So why am I repeating it? Because I still encounter those who aren't familiar with the concept or perhaps have some difficulty grasping it. I repeat it because I truly believe that life is about experiencing the effects of your choices, learning and growing from them, and appreciating the magnificence of the one law that governs the *entire* universe—ascended masters, angels, and human beings alike.

As I mentioned before, angels do not work within the confines of what makes us happy or sad, or comfortable or uncomfortable, or in terms of what we consider good or bad. These are all human constructs in which the angels cannot be contained. In obeying the law of causality, the angels are motivated by purpose and purpose alone. This is not to say they work without compassion or love—quite the opposite. It is through compassion for those of us who are brave enough to endure the trials of this human experience, and out of love for us as sisters and brothers in spirit, that the angels operate the way they do.

Because of this, should we simply live life freely and do what we please? Does living a scripted life or being bound to fate—a fate that we ourselves chose—mean that we can live our lives however we want and make decisions without fear of consequences? Or does it mean we throw up our hands in apathy and no longer continue to affect the outcome of our lives? The answer to all these questions is a firm, unequivocal *no*.

The moment we slip into apathy is the very moment we begin cheating ourselves out of learning our spiritual lessons. Though this life is scripted, our spiritual aptitude once we complete this life isn't a guarantee. Everything will happen to us just as it's supposed to, but if we give up and allow experiences to defeat us rather than empower us, then we're only racking up missed lessons that we'll have to revisit at another time. The point is that while we're here, we are obligated to do at least one of two things: learn or help someone else to learn. Therein lies the importance of our existence. We're not just here for ourselves, but for each other.

On that same note, we are responsible for our actions, which is why we can't live life all willy-nilly despite knowing that it's scripted. No matter our decisions, there are consequences. There will always be results that our actions bring about, and for them we are answerable.

Guardian Angels

According to a 2008 Baylor University survey of nearly 1,700 American adults, over half claimed they believed they were protected by guardian angels. In "Half of Americans Believe in Guardian Angels," a *Washington Times* article that highlighted the survey that same year, Rodney Stark, the co-director of Baylor University's Institute for Studies on Religion, expressed his surprise by saying he'd have guessed the number to be more around 15 percent than 55.

"This is the taboo subject in American religion. No one studies it, but there is a lot of it out there," Stark was quoted as saying in the article.

No one studies it? Where was I when this survey was being taken?

Oh yeah, fighting with Archangels Raphael and Gabriel over writing my first book *about* angels.

I have to admit that if I had been asked if I believed in guardian angels twenty years ago, I'd have keeled over laughing. I wasn't raised with a religious background that focused on angels, and I thought that people who believed in them were a little on the loopy side.

Well, guess who's joined the loopy side in the last two decades! It's not my fault; Azrael lured me over with the promise of all-you-can-eat chocolate, while Michael flashed his flawless eight pack and smirked, "You know you wanna hang with us."

Still, if anyone were to ask me today if I believed in guardian angels back then, I wouldn't laugh at them, but I would give them a firm, resounding *no*.

I understand that people still cling to the notion that an angel is watching over them. It's apparent in all the gift and card shops that sell angel pendants or greeting cards encouraging people to have faith in their guardian angels. The general consensus is that the guardian angel is supposed to protect the person from injury or misfortune. How many times have we heard a news report about someone who narrowly escaped harm and claimed that God's angels were protecting them?

It can be a comforting thought that the warrior angels like Michael, Uriel, and Cassiel are always near to shield us from calamity, hardship, the influence of sinners, or even from committing sins ourselves. But from what I have been shown by the angels themselves, such is not always the case. The angels are watching us, to be sure. But are they protecting and guarding us, as we've been led to believe for millennia?

As I mentioned in chapter 2, whatever we are to encounter during our human experience is already written in our life script. Whatever circumstances befall us are set in motion by our own free will to choose our experiences and by Heaven's trust in us to endure them. If you barely make it to a shelter before a twister tears through your town, you were meant to survive. And in this respect, the angels assigned to you were protecting you the entire time. If, however, it's written that you're to get a little banged up and bruised—or a lot—on the way, then that's what will happen. Remember, the angels are the divine custodians of fate and are obligated to bring about whatever experiences you agreed to before you were born.

I try to discourage clients, students, and readers from using the term "guardian angel," because we tend to place a lot of misallocated faith on the operative word "guardian." That is not to say we don't have angels dutifully walking beside us. From what has been revealed to me, I have observed that each human has at least two angels with them at any given time. One of these angels I already mentioned— the parent angel. The second is what I call the mentoring angel.

Your parent angel is the angel you connect with in the Realm of Spirit before you are born. This angel has made a vow to you, a contract of sorts, that he will walk by your side and see you through every life challenge you have written in your script. The parent angel is with you from the moment you take your first breath in this reality until well after you have returned home. Once back in the Realm of Spirit, the angel then reviews your life with you and discusses what lessons, if any, may need revisiting in your next life.

While reading through the angels listed in appendix C, you may feel more akin to some angels than others. If you come across an angel you feel very strongly about, chances are good that that is your parent angel. We tend to mirror our parent angel's likes and dislikes, their view of the human world, and how they may handle certain situations. In an athletic competition, for example, you may not have Metatron's view that everyone is a winner just for trying or doing their best. Instead, you may resonate more with Michael's view that there can only be one sun in the sky and you're it! (For more comprehensive profiles on angelic personalities, see my two previous works, *Azrael Loves Chocolate, Michael's A Jock* and *The Angel Code*.)

All in all, your parent angel is charged with escorting you to this reality, through it, and back home again. In a way, they're much like our spiritual chaperones.

The other angel, your mentoring angel, works with you at much closer range. But unlike your parent angel, who is with you during the course of your entire life, mentoring angels change with the seasons and cycles of your life. Depending on the lessons you must learn during a particular leg of your spiritual journey, mentoring angels will switch in and out based on that angel's area of expertise.

During an angel consultation, it is the mentoring angel that I often see for a client because that angel is directly connected to the current status of the client's life lessons. My client may feel a profound closeness with Archangel Raphael, but because of her current lessons in finding spiritual balance, Archangel Chamuel may be standing in the foreground and offering his wisdom to help her achieve that balance.

I discovered a while back how the angels switch in and out of our lives based on the circumstances we're encountering. There may be times when you feel as though they aren't there, but they are. The angels are always nearby. And while we must face the harsh notion that they're not always here to protect us, but rather to teach and guide us, I think we can still take solace in knowing that they do so with great love and compassion.

One blustery January morning, after having gone homeless as a result of my stroke and resulting complications, I found myself sitting at the local Department of Human Services. As I tuned out the sounds of a half dozen agitated infants waiting with their even more agitated mothers, I pondered which form of suicide might be the most noble. A fancier of swords and medieval weaponry, I owned a few collectible pieces that might make for one heck of a dramatic harakiri. But that would be messy. I envisioned lulling myself to sleep with a brew of hemlock and then lying upon a bed of white linen—in a white gown—whilst holding onto my collectible broadsword from the *Highlander* series. I would be surrounded by candlelight, with my stereo playing some ethereal choir music on repeat.

Aye, that would be one beautiful way to die. The thought actually brought a smile to my face.

But I was soon pulled out of the daydream as I heard a clerk call out someone's name. I cursed silently at the woman who yanked me from my fantasy back into this cold, smelly, dingy graveyard of the walking dead. *Wait, Archangel Cassiel is the patron of graveyards,* I thought. I knew I shouldn't demean such sacred places by comparing them to the office I was sitting in.

A man walked past me. He reeked of stale cigarette smoke. Dressed in a blue windbreaker, a dingy orange t-shirt, a pair of khakis that were shredded at the cuffs, and a pair of muddy tennis shoes, he schlepped up to the front desk.

"I'm looking for homeless assistance," he said, scratching at his unkempt beard.

"Are you homeless?" the clerk asked, eyeing him from over the rims of her glasses. My brow furrowed at the dim-witted question, and it took all the self-control I had not to give the clerk a glare of *Are you flippin' kidding me?*

The guy coughed harshly and choked on a gravelly "yeah."

"Where'd you sleep last night?"

"At the bus stop."

"Which one?"

"Around the corner."

"Hmm." The clerk gathered a few slips of paper and placed them on a clipboard with a pen. "Fill this out and give it back to me." The man took the forms, then shuffled through the densely packed room and sat right across from me. His hand shook as he attempted to fill out the paperwork, and I couldn't help but gaze at him. His stare looked hollow and hopeless, and his light blue eyes were ringed with red and underscored by deep, dark circles. Stringy strands of dishwater blonde hair slipped and slid everywhere. He looked as if he hadn't bathed in a while.

As I watched him, I pondered my own situation. I hadn't slept at a bus stop the night before. Actually, I hadn't slept at all, as insomnia and depression had kept me far away from any restful slumber. But the entire time I lay awake, I had been in a warm bed in a house away from the wintry elements. I had showered that morning, despite the difficulty of trying to get in and out of a shower with legs that could barely walk, much less climb over the lip of a bathtub. My hair was done and my clothes were clean.

So why the hell was I here? Oh right, for those pesky necessities called food and medication. Ah, but only moments ago, I had wanted to die. Without food or medication, death would have come soon enough. But I didn't really feel like dying on an empty stomach that day.

My mind was reeling. I wanted out of this office. I wanted out of this life! Everything in the past months had turned upside down and nothing made sense anymore. And to make it all worse, I was intuitively wide open. As I sat there begrudging my fate, I could feel the dull, grinding ache of the sorrow and hopelessness oppressing everyone around me. From the mothers trying to feed their children, to the homeless people looking for a warm place to sleep, to the elderly people trying to decide between food and medication, souls were crying out for mercy, for love, for someone to give a damn.

For God to give a damn.

My heart began to race as panic set in. I wasn't sure when I had become so antisocial or when exactly being outside of my comfort zone had created so much anxiety in me, but as the sounds of wailing children, a girl on her cell phone screaming belligerently at her boyfriend, and a homeless woman's rant foretelling the end of the world assailed me, I felt myself nearing the threshold of insanity. I closed my eyes and tried to shut out the chatter as well as the atmosphere of unmitigated spiritual agony.

"Breathe," I whispered to myself as I tried to think of something positive. It was a futile attempt. I hadn't meditated in months, and going within proved to be difficult. I dug my nails into my knees and bit my bottom lip. The mental meltdown that I'd been fearing all this time was near. I could feel it.

"Open your eyes, Chantel." Archangel Raphael, the angel of healing, and Sandalphon, the angel of love, had moved into my spiritual space. I could feel their warmth, their calming presence. Tense and shaking, I opened my eyes to see them there surrounded by a radiant white light. Immediately their angelic presence consumed me as the light expanded throughout the room.

Curiously, I watched as Sandalphon left Raphael's side to visit the play area where children tinkered with a few withered old toys. Raphael, however, stood in the midst of all of us and lifted his arms heavenward. Instantly, the tension in the office dissipated. Grim and bitter faces softened, the noise and chatter lessened, and there was a noticeable calm that settled over everyone. Even the infants stopped crying.

"Wow, everyone got quiet," the homeless man across from me chortled as he looked about.

"That's because we're all too tired to even talk," a woman a few seats down replied dryly.

I'm not sure how long Raphael held the space with his peaceful aura, but I was so grateful to him just then. I wanted to get up and hug him, but I knew that doing so would have landed me in the psychiatric ward at the nearest hospital. After all, no one but me could see the luminous angel. Or so I assumed.

After waiting an eternity to see a counselor, my name was finally called. Using a cane, I shuffled slowly to the door, greeted the woman, and followed her to her cubicle. As I sat at her desk while she typed on her keyboard, shame and anger washed over me.

This is so demeaning! Humiliating! I don't belong here! I did everything I was supposed to. I listened to my parents. I went to college. I chose career over relationships and starting a family. Damn it, I did all the right things. Why, God, why am I sitting here at this desk begging for a handout?

The thoughts came at me like a thousand arrows. I tried to shut out the images of my parents looking down upon me from Heaven with shame in their eyes. With disdain, or perhaps even disgust, knowing my father. He was never one to hide his contempt for the system and the people who used it.

"I'm sorry, Dad," I whispered to myself.

"Pardon?" The counselor swiveled in her seat and looked at me.

"Nothing," I said, offering a weak smile.

"Well, you are one lucky woman," she said as she flipped through my application. "Had you submitted this a few days earlier or a few days later, we wouldn't be able to help you."

Luck had nothing to do with it. I knew it was all part of God's plan.

"We can assist you with your prescriptions and get you some food. Do you have any children?"

"No," I said indignantly. My skin was very thin when it came to such a topic, and I knew it shouldn't have been. *Yes, a black woman can be in her thirties with a college degree and no kids!* I knew it was something I had to let go of.

"That's too bad," she sighed as she wrote notes on my application. "We could have gotten you some cash if you did."

I had been sitting on the edge of my chair, but after those words, I found myself slumping and slipping backwards. At that moment, my thirty short years passed before my eyes. Thirty years of hard work, of an undying dedication to education and earning every dollar I made. Thirty years of thinking so highly of myself … all thrown back in my face. Because I chose to go to school, because I chose to work, because I chose to do what my parents had deemed to be right and proper, I was worth no more than a few pence.

And like the dreg of society that I felt I was, I took it. It was better than nothing.

———————————————— ❧ ————————————————

Once back in my prison of a bedroom, I gazed at the altar I had set up on my bookshelf. I gazed at the many statues I had collected over the years: Buddha, Kwan Yin, Ganesh, Hotai, Fu Lu Shou. In the center of them all was a small placard depicting Merciful Jesus.

A sigh of hopeless resignation escaped me. Maudlin tears fell. Sure, he had kept his promise. My father in spirit had promised me the previous November that I would not go without my medical needs being met. At first, I scoffed at his words. There was no way I could afford the many medications, and unless there was some hidden inheritance somewhere, I knew I never would. But he came through. Just as the last of my medications ran out, there was help.

However, the now cynical and empirically bitter side of me wondered how long such a luxury would last. Time would tell.

And there, as I sat in darkness and peered at the placard, the persistent thorn in my side made its presence known—Archangel Gabriel.

"What?" I asked, without taking my eyes from the altar. To gaze at the angel would have no doubt caused me to somehow find the energy and strength to lunge at his throat.

Stoic as ever, he stood there, his hands folded in front of him. His robes were gleaming white, and his head was crowned in golden ringlets. He was flawlessly beautiful. But that harsh gaze he always seemed to wear lately evoked in me even more contempt for the militant angel. Damn, I hated him, and there were no words in the English language—short of a long string of utterly foul curses—that could convey just how deep that hate ran.

The angel said nothing—odd for him. Instead, a rush of heat came over me, and bright, vivid visions appeared before my intuitive eye. They were visions of me in the past. They began with one I remembered all too well. It was Christmas Day of 1997.

My father had just passed away a little over a month prior, and to say it was a solemn holiday season would be an understatement. As always, Mother was up early and in the kitchen, but I was feeling unglued. I didn't want to be home.

It had felt claustrophobic for weeks, and the death of my father had driven a frigid but temporary wedge between my mother and me. She had grown clingy in ways she had *never* been before, and unfortunately I had no emotional capacity to tolerate it. Though she was a good mother, a hard-working mom who cleaned, cooked, and worked upwards of sixty hours a week, she wasn't very affectionate or attentive. Instead, my father had always been the source of hugs, kisses, and unwanted curiosity about my teenage and then later adult life. Now that he was gone, the woman, who on many days chose work to get away from a family life everyone knew she didn't want, was now turning to me for something I couldn't give—closeness. Sure, it was selfish, and I regret it now, but I can't change what was.

I was desperate to find an excuse to get out of the house. Any excuse would have worked. Well, not any excuse. I could have chosen to go to a friend's house for Christmas dinner, but I wasn't that cruel. Besides, I knew Mom's wrath, and to forgo her dinner for someone else's would most likely have gotten me disowned. So instead, I wedged myself into the kitchen beside her and made small talk while I made sandwiches. A lot of sandwiches. Upwards of about three or four dozen. Maybe more. I had lost count. I made them with whatever I could find—whatever looked and tasted good— and bagged them up along with a few pounds of fruit.

"Where in the hell are you taking all of that?" she asked, eyeing me over a bowl of sweet potato pie filling.

"To the streets," I said dryly. "Be back by dinner." And I was gone. I drove downtown to one of the darkest, most godforsaken places in Detroit: Cass Corridor. It was here that most of the homeless people in the city gathered. I went to school not too far from the area, so I had become a bit desensitized to the hellish visions that lurked there. The usual cardboard boxes that served as people's homes were empty that day. It seemed that most of the people had moved into one of the many abandoned buildings to avoid the blistering cold. Still, I found a few souls brave enough to walk the desolate streets. With the holiday, the city was truly a ghost town.

I spent the afternoon handing out food and talking to total strangers, strangers who were now ghosts in my mind. I knew I would never see these people again. I also knew that such a deed would also go unrewarded by Heaven. I wasn't there to be benevolent or charitable. I wasn't there to do God's work. I was there because I felt there was nowhere else to go. It was something my mother couldn't argue against.

After a couple hours of enduring the icy winds, I returned to my car and drove to my university's campus. I walked around for a while, enjoying the haunting feeling of being the only person on the planet. The winds howled down the main corridor, and dried leaves scurried across my feet. There wasn't a soul to be found. Bundled up, I sat in the empty student square. And as I gazed at the damp leaves and wisps of ice crystals blowing across the concrete path, I broke the silence with two short sentences.

"God, why can't those people just get jobs? I have a job." Heck, before my current job that I had just gotten that past August, I had held down two part-time jobs and gone to school. It didn't seem all that difficult of a thing to do.

The vision ended there and faded into yet another of me standing in a grocery checkout line with my mother when

I was a little girl. There was a woman ahead of us with a baby on her hip and one in the front seat of the cart. She was fumbling trying to tear food stamps out of her coupon book while holding the baby.

My mother snorted in derision, "There goes my tax dollars." I looked up at her in confusion. At the time, I had no idea what she meant by that, but the angry, heated glare the woman gave my mother and the nervous look on the cashier's face always stuck with me. When the woman left, my mother started on a little tirade about my father's sister and her kids. "Shiftless, never worked a day in their lives. Never will. The entire clan is useless."

"I got a sister like that," the cashier said with a chuckle. "Got pregnant, figured out it was free money. She hasn't worked in years and here I am working and can't afford a pack of pig's feet, much less the steaks she's always eatin'."

"Well, God blesses the child that has his own." Then my mother looked at me and said, "You remember that."

The vision wavered in front of me, and this time I was a few years older and with my father. It was a nearly identical scenario, only my father had cross words for my mother's children from her previous marriage. "Stay away from those people, girl. They're all criminals, and they will only take advantage of you."

Those words didn't faze me much. I was used to him and his contempt for "those people," as he called them … on his better days. (When he was really in a foul mood, the names he reserved for them would make the Devil cringe.) It was when we got into the car that I met his wrath. And for what? I hadn't done anything wrong. But whenever my father saw a woman carting around a brood of unkempt and unruly kids,

I would become the target of his ire since he couldn't really say anything to the woman's face. No, that just wasn't gentlemanlike.

"I swear," he said as he started up the car, "if you ever come home pregnant … If I even so much as see you looking at a boy, I will skin you alive, girl, and then put you on the streets. I will not have it in my house!"

"Yessir," I responded meekly.

"Welfare is for the weak and for the do-no-gooders. Your sister ain't worked a single day in her life and look at her. Worthless!" And it was that hatred of my mother's now very distant family that drove a wedge between my parents. I could never really understand why, because she didn't have much to do with them, anyway. She had left them for another life and never looked back.

Her doing that, along with my father's contempt and derision, would cost me everything years later, including the family home and everything I owned.

I didn't have time to linger on the thought, as Gabriel ushered in another vision of me once again in the checkout line. Only now, I had my own groceries and my checkbook out and ready while staring at another woman with food stamps. Years of conditioning had worked. My parents would have been proud.

"Good grief," I scoffed at the cashier as the woman walked away. "Is it so difficult to ask people to get off their asses and work?" The cashier chuckled as she rang me up.

The vision faded, and here I was back in the darkness of my bedroom. I glanced to the copy of the application that had been approved only hours prior. In that one moment, I had become everything my parents hated.

I had become the very thing I hated.

I had no words for Gabriel, and he had none for me. After a moment, he faded into the darkness. I didn't move from my spot for hours, stuck in a vicious cycle of contempt, self-pity, and dread. Now, I would be the one to be mocked and humiliated at the checkout counter. The notion brought to me the painful realization that karma, as it were, was a rabid female Rottweiler cornering me, a pampered Persian pussycat that had pooped herself out of fear.

Here, I must be cautious. When I mention karma, I don't mean it in terms of good versus bad karma or even in the sense of retribution. Here, karma simply goes back to what I covered earlier about causality. My parents had created conditions—indoctrinating me against public assistance to the point of callous cruelty—that invariably led to my feeling too arrogant to file an application. I had been told about assistance months prior, but pride had kept me from filing for it until an empty stomach, in addition to a broken body, pushed me into action. So if, due to my upbringing, I had not been so prideful, I would have immediately submitted the paperwork. Doing so, however, would have caused me to miss the window of opportunity that allowed me to obtain services and medications I needed at the time.

Furthermore, not only did this same karma lead to the single most humbling experience in my life, but it allowed someone the opportunity to show compassion when they didn't have to. The first day I used my assistance, I rode back and forth in the electric shopping cart for a good thirty minutes. I was petrified of someone seeing me use it, of someone saying to me the heartless things my parents had said in the past, or saying to me things I myself had said to others. When I could wait no longer, I finally went through the checkout line. I couldn't even look the cashier in the face as I went to hand her my card.

"You swipe it in the machine, baby," she said as she gently took the card from me and swiped it herself. My hand was shaking so badly from fear, I couldn't do it. She walked me through the process and then went to bag my groceries.

"I never thought my life would come to this," I mumbled to myself.

"No one plans to be down on their luck, sweetheart. Just be grateful that God made a way so you can survive until you get back on your feet." There was no malice in her voice. No mocking. No ridicule. Still, I couldn't lift my head, and her words only made my eyes sting with unshed tears.

She put the last bag in my cart. "Look at me."

I swallowed hard and gripped the handle of my cart.

"Pretty please?"

When I did, her smile was warm and genuine. "Do you know how many people are going through hard times right now? You're not the only one, so don't you go hanging your head in shame. You do what you can do and let God handle everything else." She patted me on the back before returning to the register to take care of the lady behind me. I headed out of the store, and as I sat waiting for the bus—something else that was wholly foreign to me—all I could do was whisper a word of thanks to God for the compassionate souls that still roamed the earth, because there were too many like myself. Not the pathetic, self-pitying kind I had become, but the arrogant, self-righteous kind I had once been.

As dark days grew into darker months and I came to despise my circumstances with a loathing so potent that I could taste it, I became more resolute in my resolve—the moment I stepped foot in Heaven again, I was going to punch Archangel Gabriel's lights out. If I had actually scripted the horror film that was my life—something I was having trouble believing at the time—why hadn't he tried harder to stop me? Why didn't he simply say, "No, Chantel. You'll be miserable for the duration you're there." Because it is in the Realm of Spirit where we exercise our free will. It is there where we can work without all the limits and confines that we often feel in this reality. As long as we possess the mastery needed to navigate the lives we choose, no one will stop us from selecting whatever experiences we feel will increase our knowledge and understanding of ourselves.

After all, that is our ultimate goal—mastery of the self. While living this human experience, we can connect to our cosmic siblings, who will in turn help us to better understand our own human spiritual nature. From there, our knowledge expands to that of the Realm of Spirit, then to all sentient creatures, and then back to the Source. And within the Source you will find yourself, for there is where you began. There is your purest self, your higher self—unfettered, fully awake, and fully aware of all that exists within and around you.

But to get to that point, our young souls have to start somewhere, like in realities such as this one. Each human experience we have is like a class we attend for the betterment of our souls. Sure, you could take basket weaving for that easy A, but just how much would that class benefit you in the grander scheme of things? Likewise, trying to attempt computer science when you still have trouble just turning on a calculator won't net you much, either. This is why working with the archangels before we're born is so crucial—because they know and understand the nature of the Source (the collective spiritual consciousness) and Creation. Many of them have lived it themselves, so they are best suited to help us baby humans figure out what courses we should take from one semester to the next. Still, we humans are stubborn creatures, so we don't always listen to our older brothers and sisters, which is why they come along for the ride. For that reason alone, we owe them our love and gratitude.

Once here, the archangels keep their vows to help us study, as well as drill us for exams. They run us through spiritual gauntlets to prepare us for the challenges coming around the bend. So despite my rocky beginning with the archangels, I love them beyond words. They have put up with my biting words, my ungratefulness, my obstinacy. They have served as my emotional punching bags and targets of blame. They do this for all of us, and still they dutifully, lovingly remain by our side.

There are no creatures so patient and willing to put up with every ounce of vileness that humans can throw at them as the archangels. Their love is pure and unconditional. They guide us, comfort us, encourage and inspire us. And when the time is right and we have learned the lessons we set out to learn, they will lift us up and celebrate with us.

Even when they don't agree with the life scripts we write, even when they know they will be called upon to dry our tears, heal our hearts, and keep us company, they won't badger us with *I told you so* ... much. They won't disparage or mock us. And they will never, ever abandon us.

chapter four

RETURNING HOME

I sat in the parking lot watching the sun set over the trees in the distance. Transfixed by the deep, amber glow filtering through the dark leaves and over the tops of suburban houses, I allowed my thoughts to drift. This moment of silence, even for as brief as it would be, was something I needed. It was something that would hopefully quell the nervous anxiety that had gripped me days earlier and had refused to let go.

The trip down the spiral of that anxiety had begun a few days prior, in the autumn of 2006, when a client visited the store where I occasionally did readings. I had no scheduled appointments that day, but being at the store drinking tea was infinitely better than being confined to that upstairs bedroom at that godforsaken house, eating cold soup out of a can.

It was because I wasn't expecting anyone that I was surprised to see my client walk in the door, and the worry etched deep in her features set off my internal alarms. Something was horribly amiss.

For the sake of this story, we'll call her Tracy.

Tracy had always been one of my bubblier clients, always willing to share in a quip or two about "the boys"—what my clients had begun calling the archangels that I channeled for them. But that day, it seemed that all the light had been drained from Tracy's soul. Within a few minutes of getting her seated and serving her a cup of hot tea, I found out why.

Her mother was dying.

"I'm at peace with Mom leaving," she said as she held the china cup between her palms. "The family knew this was coming months ago. Mom knew. But now, as she's nearing that moment, she's afraid, Chantel. She's so scared of dying, and there's nothing I or my sisters can say to allay those fears."

I felt my stomach clench. I knew exactly what Tracy was going through, for I had just lost not only my mother in 2001, but two very close spiritual mentors as well. Over the course of four years, I had lost the three most important female influences in my life. I had even had my own brush with death thrice during that time period, so the feelings I had for Tracy and her circumstances weren't borne of mere sympathy. I was right there with her on the same page and processing my personal experiences and the emotions they evoked.

Still, there was one slight difference between us. Neither my mother nor my two spiritual mentors had ever expressed—to me, anyhow—any of the fears they may have had about their coming transition. Tracy's mother had cancer, and I had lost all three women to a form of cancer. Each of them had known well in advance what was to come, at least according to the doctors. But none of them had spoken a word to me of the impending final moment.

I remember the day my mother, Peggy, was officially diagnosed with lung cancer and given only five months to live. The two of us silently left the doctor's office, rode the elevator down to the first level, and walked out into the parking lot to face the brisk winter wind. My mom stood solidly against the wind, as if defying it. The look on her face wasn't foreign to me. She was a tough cookie and often took that tough, wide-legged stance whenever she faced adversity of some kind. I, however, was a ball of nerves. I wanted to scream, cry, wail. I wanted more tests to be taken; I wanted second opinions. I wanted to hire the best alternative physicians in the world—to do anything that would give my mother a fighting chance.

With a stoic glance around the parking lot, I saw her clench her teeth. She then reached into her purse and pulled out her cigarette case. It was something I had come to view as an extension of her. Wherever Peggy went, so did that navy blue leather case where she kept her light cigarettes tucked away, along with an emergency twenty dollar bill, a cigarette lighter, a book of matches, and old lottery tickets—some winners, some losers. She gave the case a long, hard stare. Ever since she was sixteen, she had smoked. And here at age sixty-four, a habit that I had constantly badgered her about had finally caught up to her, it seemed.

She went to extract a cigarette from the case and then stopped short. With a sigh, she closed the case and tucked it back into her purse. "For the first time, I'm not in the mood for one." She gave a dry chuckle and headed for the car.

As we drove around the small suburb, I remained quiet. She didn't seem to have any real destination in mind, which frightened me even more. It wasn't like my mom to look so lost. I could tell she was trying to hold everything together— it was just her way. And I wished I could be as strong as she seemed to be, but every now and then I had to turn my head to look out the passenger window and swipe away a tear.

To my shock, we wound up shopping that day. A lot. She shopped as if she didn't have a care in the world, and it wasn't just for clothes. She bought a couple new pieces of furniture—huge pieces that left me standing in the showroom with my jaw on the floor.

"I've been eyeing these pieces since last year. I plan on enjoying them while I can."

Nonplussed, I simply nodded.

After a few hours we found ourselves sitting at one of her favorite restaurants. And still we were both locked in silence. We hadn't said much to each other in the couple hours since the doctor's office other than to toss opinions back and forth about her unplanned shopping spree. But the silence had been too long for me. I couldn't take it anymore.

As I clutched my cup of coffee, I lifted my bleary eyes to her. No doubt they were red as I tried my best not to cry in front of her. "Mom, talk to me. Tell me what you're feeling."

"I'm feeling just fine, baby. It's God's will, so I'm rolling right along with it," she said as her eyes scanned the menu. How could she be so calm and collected? So unfazed by the literal death sentence that had been handed to her mere hours ago?

After another long pause, while I tried to sort the thoughts in my head, I finally gave voice to a question that perhaps was too soon to ask. Still, I had to know. "Do you have any regrets?" I muttered softly with trembling lips. My mother took a sip of her coffee and glanced out the window to the mid-afternoon traffic passing by.

She was quiet for so long that I didn't think she'd answer me, but after a short sigh, she finally leveled a warm, loving gaze on me. "No, baby. I've lived my life as best as I could. I've lived it to the fullest, so there are no regrets here. Not a single damn one." She smiled at me, and in that moment I saw unshed tears in her eyes. I reached my hand out to her across the table and she took it in a firm grip, a grip that could rival any man's from all the hard work she'd done all her life to raise a family.

"And I don't want you regretting anything, either," she said before the waitress came to take our order.

My mother continued to hold on to that strength up until her final moments, so when my client Tracy relayed the fear that her mother was expressing, I couldn't exactly look to my experience with my mother's death for guidance. I had to look to my own personal experience with it. I've faced death a few times in this life. Throughout childhood, I had an unnatural fear of it. So as Tracy shared the details of her mother's circumstances with me, I quickly filed through the process that helped me to move past that fear.

Tracy actually pinpointed the solution before I could. She lifted her eyes that shimmered with unshed tears and asked, "Will you come talk with her and tell her about the angels?"

Yep, that was it. It was my connection with the angels that helped me to overcome the paralyzing fear of death that had all but overtaken my life by the time I reached college. Seeing the angels with my own eyes, talking with them and learning all that they were willing to teach about spirituality, moved me past the fear and into a sense of peace I never thought I'd have.

Without hesitation, I took Tracy's hand and gave it a firm squeeze. "Just tell me when and where," I said boldly. Tracy then gave me all the information and a time that would be good to visit her mother. Naturally, the sooner the better. And up until Tracy left, I'd felt confident that I might be able to help her mother find the same peace the angels had given me.

That confidence crumbled the instant Tracy left the store. After a moment of thinking through what I had just consented to, I fell into a state of panic. To do consultations for clients and connect them with their angels was one thing, but to sit with someone who was standing on the very threshold between life and death and talk about angels was a whole different thing. As always with me, that tiny fraction of me that remains a skeptic, the part of me that defiantly stands before the angels during my personal conversations with them and says, "Yeah, I'll believe it when I see it," reared its ugly head.

There, as I stood in the shop alone, that one sliver of doubt in my mind that I can never seem to let go of said, *What if you're wrong?* My breath hitched and I began to pace the floor. What if the angels were all a part of my imagination? What if they didn't really exist and I was just some crazy lady hearing voices? *What if?*

With a deep groan, I sat down and covered my face with my hands. I wanted to call Tracy right then and there and cancel the appointment, but how low of a human did I have to be? I couldn't just toss the matter aside.

"Stop panicking," Archangel Raphael said as he appeared before me. Dressed all in white and holding onto his shepherd's staff, he gazed at me with large brown eyes as a golden aura radiated around him.

"I can't do this, Raphael. I mean, what do I say to her?" I clutched at the roots of my hair as all kinds of scenarios played out in my mind, right down to the ghost of the woman coming back to haunt me for misleading her about the other side.

"*You* don't say anything," he said, pointing a long finger at me. "Let me handle it."

I scoffed at the archangel with a chuckle. "Right. Whatever you say, chief." Hey, if he wanted to take the reins on this, fine. The internal paradox was heavy enough to crush me. On one hand, I was too skeptical of the angels and my own gifts to connect with them to keep the appointment. On the other, I was too much of a coward to face the woman and so would hide behind this archangel—real or imagined—and see what happened.

Irrational thinking? Of course it is. I knew that then and I know that now, but there was so much that was still so new to me that I really didn't know how to approach the situation. If nothing else, I would go and offer comfort the best way I could. I would treat her as if she were my own mother, with respect and love, and maybe, just maybe, that would be enough.

All of that brought me to the moment where I was sitting in the parking lot of the very same hospital where I had been treated for pneumonia earlier that year; only now, instead of panicking over a bill I couldn't pay, I was panicking over the spiritual task I had agreed to carry out. I felt so ashamed! I felt like a sham. A fraud! Other than talking to the angels directly and connecting with clients who claimed that my consultations were accurate, I had not a single shred of proof that my spiritual life had a basis in reality. With a sigh, I pounded my head against the steering wheel.

"God, I really don't want to do this," I whispered.

"Which part of 'you don't have to do anything' did you not understand?" Raphael spoke, and I looked up in the rearview mirror to see him sitting in the back seat. "Come on, let's go."

Reluctantly, I gathered my things and got out of the car. Within minutes, I was walking into the hospital room where Tracy, her sister, her brother, and her mother were. I'll call her mother Gladys.

For someone with only days to live, Gladys looked incredibly well. Her eyes were bright and she was smiling. For a moment I thought perhaps I had entered the wrong room, at least until Tracy got up to greet me. She introduced me to her sister, who expressed that she wanted to get a consultation with me in the near future. And then Tracy turned me to her brother, who gave me a disdainful lookover. It was a skeptical look I knew well, as if he couldn't believe his sister would bring some storefront psychic to sit with his mother in her last days. I didn't fault him for feeling that way. If I had been in his shoes, I would have most likely felt the same way considering the skepticism I had about myself and the angelic world I was still learning so much about.

"Do you want us to leave the room?" Tracy obviously caught on to the contempt her brother was exuding, but I declined her suggestion.

"No, you can all stay," I said and went to take a seat by Gladys. She offered her hand to me and I took it. It was cool, but very soft. She was a graying woman, looking to be in her seventies, but I could tell by the light in her eyes that she still had a lot of spunk. If she were to leave soon, the angels would have to drag her away. She had the look of a woman who still had so much more she wanted to do.

"My daughter says you talk to the angels," she said with a smile. There was no skepticism in her features. Her demeanor was open and welcoming, and she treated me with a reverence that I didn't in the least feel I deserved. If anything, I really wished the family had called a priest instead. The mangled soul that I was was hardly fit to help someone transition from this side to the other, but there was no backing down now. I was locked in for the ride.

"Either that or I need to be wrapped up in a straightjacket and tossed into a padded cell," I chuckled lightly.

Gladys laughed boisterously and with more vigor than I expected from someone in her condition. "Good, we can be roommates then," she said good-naturedly. I couldn't help but laugh, too, and I was grateful to Heaven that she was in such high spirits. She seemed to be in much better spirits than Tracy had initially implied, and I was left wondering how to broach the topic of the reason I was there. Luckily, I didn't have to. It seemed that Raphael had started the show without me.

"Well, I don't think you're crazy in the least bit," Gladys began. "My daughter told me you were coming, and at first I laughed her out the room about bringing a psychic to see me. No offense."

"None taken," I smiled.

"But then I got a visit." She breathed deeply to continue her sentence, and that's when Raphael appeared and tapped me on the shoulder.

"Tell her I'm here," the archangel said, and then he went to stand over by the door. I swallowed hard and braced myself, knowing not to dawdle when it comes to angelic instruction. Before Gladys could say another word, I gave her hand a gentle squeeze.

"Hold on just one second, Gladys. I don't mean to interrupt you, but..." I glanced up a moment at Tracy and her siblings sitting over by the window. Her brother didn't seem too interested in what was happening and had his eyes plastered to the game show on television. "Archangel Raphael just told me to inform you that he's here."

Tracy and her sister gasped. Her brother let out a sound of disgust. It was Gladys's reaction, however, that floored me. With not an ounce of surprise on her face, she pointed over at the door directly at the angel.

"I know, that's what I was gonna say. Raphael's with me now. He's standing right over there by the door." I had to sit back in my chair as my gaze slid back and forth between the woman and the angel. They were looking directly at each other!

Clearing my throat and shaking off the chill that had just washed over me, I shifted in my chair again. This had to be a coincidence. It had to be. Never had I encountered anyone who could validate my own vision of any angel so clearly. And as if Raphael knew of my apprehension, he waved at Gladys.

She waved back.

My heart began to race. I turned fully to her now even as Raphael crossed the room to stand at the foot of her bed. "Just out of curiosity, Gladys," I began with a quaking voice, "how does he appear to you?"

"Well, he's tall," she said. That was a no-brainer. Most accounts of the angels often begin like that. "He's wearing all white." Again, nothing to write home about. "He's got long brown hair and dark eyes and he's holding a staff." My eyes slid to the archangel standing at the foot of the bed. His features were stoic and betrayed no emotion. I was rendered speechless.

"I'll tell you, Chantel," Gladys whispered, "if I'd known the angels were that good-lookin', I'd have left out of here a long time ago." She gave me a sly smile and elbowed me. I was in too much shock to respond, but Raphael actually seemed to blush as he glanced down at his feet. She shook my hand to get my attention. "I'm not afraid anymore," she said finally with conviction in her voice. "I'm ready."

I gently withdrew my trembling hand and sniffed back tears. I could only nod to acknowledge her declaration even as I watched Raphael slowly fade from sight. "Thank you," I spoke to him with my mind.

"Her legs are bothering her," he whispered. "Why don't you give her some Reiki before you go?"

Again, I nodded and then looked to Gladys. "Would you like some Reiki?" I asked her and then explained to her what the alternative energy healing method encompassed.

"Oh, yes!" she smiled a bit and then groaned. "My legs are aching so bad. Will that help?"

At that point, all I could do was pat her gently on the arm, get up, and go to the foot of the bed where Raphael had been standing. I gently placed my hands on her feet. "Close your eyes and relax," I whispered, and she did just that. By time I was done administering the Reiki as per Raphael's instructions, Gladys was snoring peacefully.

Tracy and I both giggled through our tears and tiptoed out of the room to talk in the hallway. As she thanked me for the visit, I couldn't help but express my abundant gratitude to her and her mother for one of the most profound spiritual experiences of my life. Even as we stood there, I was still shaking in awe of what I'd witnessed. I had gone into the room steeped in doubt and come out believing more in the angels than I ever had before.

And I wasn't the only one. I had noticed that when I was done with the Reiki, the brother had made himself absent. On the way to the elevator, I saw him pacing slowly in the lobby. I offered him a sympathetic nod, but before I could get on the elevator, he stopped me.

"I'm not sure what happened back there, but thanks. I've not seen my mom that happy since all this began," he muttered as he looked everywhere but at me. I gave him a soft smile and patted him on the shoulder.

"I didn't do anything. The angels did it all. I was just there to watch them in action, just like you were." With that, I offered him my hand and he took it in a firm grip before we exchanged farewells. Not long after, I found myself sitting in my car again, this time staring at the starry night sky. I was still in shock over what I'd just witnessed, and as I sat there, I turned my eyes toward the massive hospital complex and wondered how many others were connecting with their angels like Gladys was. How many people were lying in their rooms, clutching their blankets and fearing their final moments, only to be soothed by the presence of an archangel?

"When it's my time…" I whispered in the silence of my car.

"We'll be there, Chantel," Raphael's voice echoed in my mind, and I then felt the warmth of his hand on my shoulder. His soothing touch moved me into such a state of calm that I didn't feel up to driving just yet. Instead, I sat there in the parking lot and gazed at the stars thinking of every soul that was leaving this planet at that moment and how each one was being escorted away in the arms of an angel.

It was a heady musing, one on which I couldn't help but superimpose all the moments when I had sat beside someone's deathbed, and even my own harrowing moments when I had thought the next breath would be my last.

———————————— ❦ ————————————

When that moment does come—however it comes—we all go through the same process. The belief that a person's life passes before their eyes is accurate. There is always the rapid flickering of memories—the person's life in review. Then immediately afterward comes the arrival of one or more "luminous beings," as they have been called by the many people who have had a near-death experience (NDE). These luminous beings could be loved ones or angels, or they could be ascended masters such as Jesus, Mary Magdalene, or Buddha.

Regardless of whether a person passes peacefully during sleep or in a tragic car accident, there will always be a representative from the Realm of Spirit there to calm, comfort, and guide the soul back home. My spirit guide Jake suffered a sudden and fatal injury while working late one night. When he died, he didn't realize it until he saw his friends and coworkers gathered around his body. At first he thought it was someone else who was hurt, but then he heard everyone yelling and screaming his name. When he looked over the shoulder of one of his coworkers and into his own face, panic and confusion set in. Such a reaction is common for those who leave in this manner.

Dutifully, Archangel Raphael was the angel who appeared by Jake's side to guide him home. Needless to say, the boy didn't want to go. He was young, not quite thirty, and just beginning to make a name for himself in his field. While he was reluctant to walk into the light with the archangel, he finally acquiesced after realizing his begging and pleading would not change anything.

Whereas Jake mentioned walking through a doorway of bright blue, shimmering light, many people who have had an NDE have described walking through a long tunnel toward a light. Still other souls have expressed that it was just like waking up from a long, detailed dream. Regardless of the path they walk to get to the other side, there is one common thread among those who pass from this world to the next: peace. There is always a sense of peace that overcomes the soul when it realizes there is nothing to fear. The general consensus is that there's a sense that everything is going to be all right—not just for the soul, but also for those being left behind.

That's the general consensus among people who have had an NDE and souls I've connected with, such as my mom and my spiritual mentor Ella. But there's always that minority of people who fight death with everything they have. Jake told me that if he hadn't felt so mentally drained from being overworked, he probably would have fought Raphael right there on the spot. But he was so tired and confused that he followed the angel with only a few heated words of protest.

"Besides, it's sorta hard to fight someone when you're butt naked," Jake said with a sheepish grin one night while we were talking by candlelight.

"You were naked when you crossed over?" I asked, leaning in closer to him.

"So embarrassing," he groaned. "I think they do that to disarm those of us who will put up a fight."

"Yikes. I thought you'd at least be in a white robe or something."

"Nope," he said as he rolled his fingers through the dancing flame. "The white robes are just a device that artists use."

"Well, I'm glad to see you got your clothes back," I chuckled.

He gave me a sidelong glance with a dry "thanks."

As someone who could pass for Archangel Cassiel's twin, Jake wore black from head to toe—a black leather biker jacket, tank top, jeans, and biker boots. If the angels hadn't given him any clothes, I can't say I would have objected. The boy wasn't hard on the eyes at all. Of course, if the boot were on the other foot, I'd be screaming in horror if I had to run around Heaven naked. Though I'm sure if Archangel Michael had his way, we would all be naked in Heaven. I haven't said it in previous books for fear of a backlash, but the Master General of the angelic armies is the patron of nudists. *Au natural* is the only way for him. Yes, I'm talking about the legendary "I kicked Lucifer's butt and got a trophy for it" Archangel Michael. There's no greater exhibitionist than him, and Sandalphon has even teased that the reason Lucifer had to go is because Heaven wasn't big enough for the colossal egos that both he and Michael have.

But I digress.

So as Jake was walking around naked and sorting through his emotions while trying to arrive at an acceptance of his fate, something very interesting was still happening to him in the human realm.

His body was in the hospital having emergency surgery in what doctors hoped would save his life. It was only the day after the incident that Jake was pronounced dead. By then, his soul had already visited loved ones and he had gotten enough of his bearings to remember, "Oh yeah, that was all just a dream. *This*, where I am now, is reality."

This little piece of information regarding my spirit guide already being gone hours before he was pronounced dead shocked me to my core. I didn't discover it until I began doing research for this book and it came up in conversation with Jake.

"Why didn't you bring this to my attention years ago?" I grumbled at him.

"You didn't seem to be fazed by it, so I thought you might have known something I didn't," he shrugged. No, spirit guides aren't always savvy about spiritual matters. They are, after all, humans training to be guides.

Though I didn't know about the phenomenon of a soul vacating the body while still alive where Jake was concerned, I had become very much aware of it with my mother in her final stages.

Mom had lung cancer with metastasis to the brain. She had become bedridden immediately after being diagnosed, because she had problems walking and was often assailed by mild seizures. And I crumbled emotionally as I watched this strong, independent woman become confined to a bed, tethered by IV tubes and monitor wires.

"Chantel, it is your destiny to teach and heal," I heard God whisper in a faint and distant memory that had been haunting me since I began college.

I clenched my eyes shut and placed my hand to my mother's head as she lay there in bed. I had no idea what to do or how to do it. I just knew I was not ready to lose her so early in my life. I felt I still had so much more to learn from her.

"You're a woman now. You're going to be just fine," Mom spoke.

"Mom, I can't help it. I don't want to lose you."

"You're not losing me, child."

It was then that my eyes popped open and I realized that my mother was still very much unconscious. She had fallen into a coma just days prior, but hearing her voice so clearly made me forget that for a moment. And then I saw her, standing bedside next to Jake, both of them smiling at me.

I broke into sobs and turned away.

"No, Mom. Don't do this. Don't go. Please." I held her cold and unresponsive hand. Still, in my mind's eye I could see her watching me. She was so young and radiant. And though I wept, she never lost her smile, as if she were patiently waiting for me to release my selfishness and let her go.

"I'm not leaving you, Chantel. I will be with you until you get back on your feet."

"Until? What about *always*?"

"You'll understand what I mean later."

"Jake, no. Stop her, please! If you want to be my guide and guardian, help me! If God wants me to heal others, tell him to show me how and make me a believer. Heal my mother!" I was on my feet and yelling at the air in the room. I then crumbled and, like a child, crawled into my mother's hospital bed and held her tight until a nurse gently pulled me away an hour or so later.

Mom passed away two days after that.

The night of her passing left me feeling numb. I returned home to the darkness of the family room as I had so many nights before, as I had the night Jake first came to me. I turned on the television to keep the tears at bay for a while, but after an hour or so, I looked up into the dark dining room to see my mother standing there, still smiling.

"You know, most people just go to Heaven when they die," I growled at her in spite. Yes, I was very angry, and much like a spoiled brat, I wanted either all of her or none.

"I told you I would be here until you got back on your feet, Chantel."

"I'll be fine." My words were clipped. "Enjoy your vacation." I turned off the television and headed upstairs.

"I love you," she whispered.

"I know. Good night, Mom."

As I look back on those instances with Jake and my mother, as well as on my research into those who have had an NDE, I've come to call the moment when the soul separates from the body the "twilight period." Twilight is the blue hour, the cusp between day and night. That moment when the soul leaves the body but has not moved on to the Realm of Spirit is the cusp between life, as we humans know it, and death. For those who have an NDE, it's that moment when they review their lives and see loved ones, angels, and even those who are still living in the human realm. Invariably, the soul is told by luminous beings that now isn't the time to cross over and hence must return to the realm of the living.

But for those who must move on, there is first the moment of denial, followed by the moment of reconciliation and peace, after which they are gently guided back home to the Realm of Spirit.

Originally, I was going to write here that some souls go on to Heaven and then later may return to connect with loved ones. At least, that's how I perceived it to be with Jake and my mother. But Jake informed me that time works so differently between the realms that what I perceived as a few hours between my mother's death and her contacting me would have seemed like days, if not longer, to her.

And there are moments when the opposite occurs. Archangel Gabriel has told me that, in general, eighty-five human years is only about a fifteen-minute dream. Why the paradox? The answer is easy: Time is an illusion. It can become whatever our minds want it to be. This is why "time flies when you're having fun," or it seems to stand still when you're anxiously awaiting news. Five minutes is five minutes, but it can seem to rush by or drag on, depending on how we feel and how we perceive the world around us.

Regardless, Mom wouldn't be the only one I'd receive a visitation from directly after her passing.

One afternoon in the spring of 2004, the phone in my office rang.

"Hello, this is Chantel," I chirped.

"Hey, hon. It's Britt."

I knew by the sound of the tears in my friend's voice what had happened. My spiritual mentor Ella had passed away just moments ago. I was stuck at work for the day, but maybe that was for the best. Britt and I talked briefly, and when I hung up the phone, I sobbed. Dabbing at my tears, I closed my office door, told the receptionist to hold my calls, and simply sat at my desk.

"Ella, I'm lying to myself. I really need you here. I don't know if I can do this all by myself." I was thinking back on all the spiritual skills she had helped me to hone, including my intuition, Reiki, and meditation.

"Why would you think I'm leaving you, baby?" Ella's voice was soft and I could see her in my mind's eye walking into my office as casually as a coworker.

"It's not the same. Besides, how do I know you're real and just not my imagination?"

"Chantel," she said as she sat at my desk, "I can't believe after everything I've taught you that you would even doubt this moment. What is it going to take for you to believe that you have a gift?"

"A lot more than voices and an overactive imagination." I sniffled and kept my voice low just in case someone out in the hall heard me talking to *no one*.

"Ella, I've had to deal with this for years." Jake said as he approached the desk. Then I broke into even more tears, as seeing him made me think of the times he'd been there when my mother had passed away.

"You gotta be joking. I don't need both of you cramping my thoughts. Isn't there medication for this?" I whined.

"See what I mean?" Jake huffed and folded his arms. I sniffled and looked at the two of them as they stared right back at me. A moment of silence passed before I threw up my hands in surrender.

"Oh, good grief! Ella, this is Jake, the spirit guide I told you about. Jake, this is Ella." I sighed and blew my nose as I casually gestured between the two of them. And as one would expect, they shook hands in pleasant greeting. I, however, had a sinking feeling very reminiscent of when my mother had come to a parent-teacher conference when I was in grade school.

"She's always been this stubborn?" Ella asked as she stood and leveled a stern gaze at me.

"She's getting better, thanks to you. But yeah, it's not been easy between the two of us." Jake grumbled a bit.

"Okay, I can hear you two! You said I have a gift. Well, I'm using it!" I was damn near frantic and felt cornered by not one but two powerful spirits now. And as if to add kerosene to the brush fire, they pulled away to the corner of the room and whispered between themselves. I couldn't hear much of what Jake was saying, but I imagine it was a lengthy report, as all I heard were Ella's responses of, "Yep. Mm hmm. Really, now? Oh, that will stop. I'll see to it. She what? No, we'll cut that out, too."

I just sank in my office chair, feeling that any moment I was going to be sent to the principal's office. At one point during their conversation I just felt the need to interject "tattletale!" at Jake, to which he laughed and disappeared with a farewell.

"Ella, she's all yours," were his last words.

That's when I lowered my head in defeat, as I not only heard Ella giggle wickedly but saw her rubbing her hands together like a villain in an old, silent film.

"Okay, fine. So I'm a skeptic. I have a right to be, you know. You want me to believe all this stuff? Fine, Ella, prove it!" I was fuming at that point and couldn't have cared less if anyone outside my office heard me arguing with *no one*.

"Easy. Look for a rainbow. That's my sign to you."

"A rainbow?"

"A rainbow."

"Riiiight. Fine. Okay, I'll look for one." I said flippantly, and Ella disappeared slowly with a grumble, something to the effect of, "I'll fix that little red wagon of yours, young lady."

Later that afternoon, I called my friend Britt to see how she was holding up. Naturally, I asked if there was anything I could do for the family hour and memorial. She asked if I would stop by the bookstore and pick up a journal so people could write their condolences, but more importantly, their memories and stories about Ella. Britt would later give the journal to Ella's sons. Thinking that was a wonderful idea, I made it a personal quest.

The day of the wake, I found myself standing at the local bookstore looking over their selection of journals. I chose one that was simple and earthy—nothing too frilly for her boys. But then I thought an engraved bookplate would add just the right touch, so off to the shopping mall engraver I went. To my relief, the bookplate would only take a few minutes to make. During that time I wandered around the store and looked over the figurines and knickknacks offered there. I finally came upon a table of pens, and it dawned on me that if we were going to have a journal, we should also have a special pen to go with it. So, in a time crunch, I circled the table with hopes that the engraver could engrave the pen as well.

Well, being the picky person that I am, I had circled the display table twice, seeing nothing that spoke of Ella really. "Ella, this is your life, your journal. *You* pick the pen!"

"Look down right in front of you." I heard her voice softly, and to my amazement, there was the most beautiful iridescent rainbow pen I had ever seen. I beheld it like Indiana Jones would a sacred treasure.

"Heh, funny," I said to myself and grabbed two pens, one for the boys and one for Britt. That evening at the funeral home, I spoke to Britt quietly about the rainbow sign and showed her the pens while handing her the engraved one and leaving the plain one out for everyone else to use. I laughed off the coincidence, but could have sworn I felt Ella's eyes bore holes right through me. But what was I to do? It was a pen that just so happened to be the color of a rainbow. No big deal, right?

———————————— ❧ ————————————

Clutching a handkerchief tight in one hand and my purse in the other, I entered the church on the day of Ella's funeral to a corridor full of Ella's friends and family. There was no question that the woman was deeply loved, but the gathering had a dual atmosphere. We all were mourning the loss of one of the most incredible women we would ever know, but at the same time we were scared witless of the power she now possessed on the other side. Many of us spiritual slackers who didn't live up to Ella's standards while she wasn't looking were about to pay dearly, and I knew I was one of them. After all, at how many funerals do you get the comment, "We are so screwed now that Ella doesn't have to sleep or stop to eat and can move at light speed. She'll never know a day's rest and neither will we." We all wept in sadness and groaned in dread of the fire Ella was about to light under all of us. Not only did the women of the tea shop realize this, but so did Ella's children.

We all joked about it as we stood in the corridor before the funeral, but suddenly her second-eldest son said, "Chantel, take a few steps back."

Caught off guard by the request, I frowned, shrugged, and stepped back. "What? Hop on one foot now?" I playfully teased.

"No, you're standing in a rainbow." He and his fiancée chuckled and pointed. I looked straight up at a stained glass window overhead as the sun was shining directly through the center of it, casting rainbows on the floor all around me. I chuckled back, "How cute," and quickly excused myself to find the ladies of the tea house.

"Did you guys tell anyone about the rainbows?" I whispered as we stood in line to enter the chapel.

"No, did you?" they all whispered back to me. The rainbow sign was certainly no secret, but I didn't know whether to dismiss the second rainbow as another coincidence or just as one of Ella's sons playing a joke.

The service in the chapel was a tearful one. The procession was led by the Eagle Scouts, for Ella was a den mother and avid supporter of her boys. A sermon from the pastor soon followed, his message focusing on being of service to others, something that came as second nature to Ella. The pastor recounted his visits to Ella while she was ailing.

"Pastor, what will that moment be like?" Ella had asked him. As I sat in the church pew, I couldn't help but shudder in fear. Ella had been my adopted mother and spiritual mentor for several years. It was under her tutelage that I had been able to hone my natural gifts of intuition. It was her wisdom that had brought to me the deeper understanding of Reiki. And it was her love that had helped me to have faith in myself as a child of spirit, a child of God.

So to hear the pastor on the day of her funeral lay bare her fears of death was a bit disconcerting. Other than my mother—who could go up against a raging bull with a terry-cloth dish towel and win—Ella had been one of the strongest women I'd ever known in mind, body, and spirit. She was a power to be reckoned with, and if ever my life had felt like a supernatural Hollywood movie, it was during the times I had spent with Ella up at her tea shop. Those times were many, and I had grown to respect and love her. I cherished every wise word she had said.

"Ella," the pastor spoke, "I know that when that moment comes, all of God's angels will be there to receive you." He then chuckled through his tears and said, "Ella leaned close to me, eyed me with scrutiny, and whispered, 'How do you know?'" The sadness in the crowd momentarily broke with the sound of laughter. Yep, that was Ella, all right. She was one tough cookie.

The pastor then looked at each of us with a lingering gaze and began to unfold his pastoral towel.

"A lot of people call this a scarf, but it's not, actually. We call this a towel and we wear it in semblance of Jesus's service to his disciples. It actually represents the towel he used to wash the feet of his disciples. I haven't worn this one in a very long time, but for some reason, I felt that it would mean something special to you all." The unfolded towel revealed a large rainbow across its midsection. He ceremoniously placed it around his neck, smoothed it out, and then looked at it lovingly. "Yes, I think Ella would have liked this one best."

It was at that moment that all of us ladies from the tea house looked to each other in complete disbelief.

"Did you see that, or am I dreaming?" whispered one of the tea shop regulars as we walked down the corridor toward the church dining hall after the service.

"I think a little bit of both," I said, feeling ill. Seeing a third rainbow was beyond coincidence; it was just plain freaky. And if that weren't enough, when all of us entered the dining hall, we came face to face with a huge rainbow painted on the wall. None of us at the tea shop had ever been in this church before, which was obvious by the look of astonishment on all of our faces.

"Oh, isn't that rainbow beautiful? The children just finished painting that the other day," said a parishioner who was passing by, leaving us standing there in a cloud of awe and wonder.

As a medium, I've connected with those who were in the process of passing, those in the twilight, and those who had already crossed over, but I think that no encounter was so pain-filled as that of my father during what I can only surmise was his twilight. Unlike my mother and Ella, my father chose to contact me in a very different way upon his passing in November of 1997.

The spring morning was sunny but still carried with it the bitter chill of winter. As I sat in the car to let it and my hands warm up with the revving engine, I meditated on the windshield wipers as they cleared away the morning's dew from my window.

"Now, baby, you take care of her and she'll take care of you. Always check your tires, and check your oil every three thousand miles, okay? Make sure your spare has air in it, and always keep spare change for a phone call," my dad rambled on as he pointed to every relevant gauge in yet another short course in car care. Yeah, as if I hadn't gotten it all the first few hundred times.

Dad was an older gent, his eighty-five years to my twenty-four at the time, and I was his only living child. He had had a family before he met my mom, but had lost his daughter to suicide, his son to friendly fire in Vietnam, and his wife to colon cancer, all within a three-year span. So when my parents met and I showed up as an unexpected bonus to their growing love, my dad married my mom and showered me with everything a young, spoiled urban princess could ever want. My pampered childhood was lush and glorious, but then came puberty, boys, and a loathing for my dad's smothering tendencies. There wasn't a moment when I didn't think I would die of sheer suffocation from the man's overprotection; my every departure from the house was preceded by questioning that could rival Homeland Security protocol.

Dad had just been finishing up his auto checklist when a white sedan pulled up beside us. A bearded man emerged from the driver's side and began to approach our car, hailing my dad's attention.

"Stay here," my father said, cautiously placing his hand on mine. With that, he exited the car and met the bearded man halfway. I turned off the engine to better hear their conversation, only to hear my father bellow curses that bounced off the bricks of the neighboring houses. Composed, the stranger returned to his car and departed. My heart pounding in fear for my father and for the man he had just verbally accosted, I emerged from my car and stood on the sidewalk.

"Dad, you can't just go around cussin' people out these days. Folks got guns, you know."

"Yeah, well, I got a shotgun."

"Who was that, anyway?"

"No one."

I stared at my dad a long moment, shrugged, and then headed up the driveway to the house. Dad was on my heels the whole time, grumbling angrily. He had a temper that could make the Devil break a sweat, so I continued walking and was not about to press the issue further.

Ominous storm clouds crept in somewhere between the first step into the house and the fourth step up into the kitchen. Bewildered, I lifted the curtains over the sink and gazed out. The sky had been so serenely blue only moments earlier.

"You sure you have to leave?" my father said, still standing at the door and looking out to those rolling clouds as well. The question sent a chill over my shoulders. Dad was a strong, overbearing man with a deep, resounding voice, but at that very moment with that very question, he sounded more like a frightened toddler.

"Yeah, I'm late, Dad." I glanced at the clock on the stove. It was eight thirty. Oddly, I wasn't exactly sure where I was headed. My response had been automatic. After years of tolerating the demands of an elderly man who now couldn't remember if he had already asked me the same question four times, I had made it my business to just not be home anymore. Whether it was school or overtime at work, there was always one reason or another for me to leave at eight in the morning and not return home until well past midnight.

"Oh. Well, okay. I love you," he muttered, and I turned to find him standing behind me with his arms open. I blinked hard once and then again. Afflicted with Alzheimer's, Dad was hardly affectionate anymore. Sure, I remember bouncing on his knee when I was a little girl, but those days were long gone and the most affection we ever exchanged was the typical "be careful" and "see you later." Regardless, I slipped into his arms, and they were warm—warm, strong, and protective like I remembered from my childhood. That hug was what I wanted from him more than anything, not his all-points checklists on cars, nightclubs, or boyfriends. I just wanted his affection again. Better late than never, I supposed.

He kissed me on the forehead and turned away, heading back out the door. "I love you, Chantel."

"I know. I love you too, Dad." I could barely get out the words as I forced back tears. I looked to the clock on the stove again. It was still frozen on eight thirty.

And then I woke up. When I glanced at the clock, it was more like ten to nine and I was grossly late for work. I sprang from bed, grabbed my clothes, and whipped past my mother with an "I'm late!" instead of a kiss good morning.

Shower be damned, I dressed as quickly as I could, cursing the whole time. To make matters worse, my half-brother wanted to vie for the bathroom I was in because the second upstairs bathroom at the back of the house only had a tub without a shower.

"What!" I barked in response to his pounding on the door.

"Call in late. The nursing home just called. They sent Buddy to the hospital." That's what my half-siblings called my dad, "Buddy." He had told them that he would never try to replace their father, but he did want to be their friend, and so "Buddy" it was. I called my dad that too, but if I wanted something, princess mode kicked in and it was always "Daaaddyyyy." And like magic, my dad would automatically reach into his pocket for his wallet and ask, "How much is this gonna cost me?"

That's exactly what I was thinking as I raced to get ready for work: how much it was going to cost me to miss a day at a job that was only two months old. "Can't you go? I can't call in late!" I shrieked back at my half-brother.

"No, *you* need to go with Mom."

The emergency room of the city hospital was packed with patients and security alike; getting in to see my father was harder than getting on an airplane as we passed through security checks along the way. When the nurse escorted Mom and me to a family room, my heart froze and I watched my mother slowly crumble as we waited for some-one to come talk to us.

The doctors entered the room. The visit was too brief for my liking, but what more could they say? My father had suffered a blood clot to the heart, or so they thought. *He was eighty-five, why bother with details?* I imagined them thinking as they departed. After a long cry with Mom and our last visit to my dad in the ER, there was only one detail that really stuck with me the rest of the day: the doctors pronounced my father's passing at exactly eight thirty.

Unlike in my dream, however, it wasn't spring. We were in the middle of a brutal, wintry November. The chill seemed degrees colder than normal, and the winds were perpetually antagonistic. Dad died right in the middle of it all, Heaven bless him, and there was no other time that I listened to him more than right then. Once on the day he died and then twice or so at the funeral, I heard his voice.

"Don't bother coming to the grave, Chantel. I'm not there. You hear me? I won't be there."

The inclination to disagree with him never came. For a while I thought my aversion to cold weather had made my cooperation easier, but even as spring arrived, I never went. During the passing seasons, my thoughts were more on the dream of my father than the death of him. Suddenly the dream became more than a flash of memories past. It was my father's final goodbye and I will forever cherish the moment.

Yet, as I sit here sixteen years later thinking back on that dream, I can't help but go back to that moment when my father was so angry and belligerent at the man in the white car. Though I was afraid to admit it to myself for years, I always thought the man looked very much like Jesus. And the thought made me cringe and whisper to the heavens, "Dad, what were you thinking?"

But my father's mind had been ravaged by Alzheimer's. I'd like to think that during his twilight hour, he was just as confused as he was frightened. To this day, I'm unsure how his moment of transition truly went, being that I haven't had any real, substantial contact with him since. The same went for my mother, too, until one day when I went looking for her on the other side.

That Sunday in the spring of 2004 was a quiet one at the tea shop. I sat reading a book as friends of the store stopped by to pay respects to my ailing Reiki Master, Ella, and her closest friend, Britt. After a long and emotionally heavy day, Britt sat down next to me with a sigh, and I felt the need to relay my experiences with Mom and Jake in hopes that it would help her to better handle Ella's passing when it came.

Knowing my mother was always close, whether real or imagined, helped me through the mourning process. We would talk in my dreams as if she had never left, and amazingly, we were able to tie up quite a few loose ends between the two of us. Still, exactly three years later, there was an emptiness inside of me, a part of me that yearned for her to be physically near.

"I know Ella is going to watch over you and the store," I said to Britt with teary eyes, "just like my mom watches over … me." And that's when I felt an emptiness much more profound than I had ever felt before. Mom was gone. I closed my eyes to call to her only to hear and see nothing. I tried to reach out to her with my soul, and still nothing. Britt, seeing that I was instantly overwhelmed with grief, placed her hand on my shoulder.

"She's gone," I choked. Just as a mother eases away from her child who has slipped quietly into slumber, so did my mom's presence leave me, silent and unnoticed.

"Oh, Chantel. She's there," Britt said, trying to console me.

"No, she's gone. She's not there!" My eyes were still closed as I searched the darkness of my intuitive vision for her. "She's ... back here. It's almost as if ..." I regrouped slowly.

"As if what?" Britt prodded.

"Nothing. I think she's been reborn." I chuckled through tears, hiding the pain in my heart. I knew at that moment what had happened. My mother felt it safe to leave my side because Ella was returning to the Realm of Spirit to watch over the next phase of my life. The notion was only proven to be true when Ella passed away just days later.

It wouldn't be until I had gone on a tour of the Realm of Spirit with Archangel Gabriel that I would encounter my mother again. It was when the angel and I passed through the Akashic Records that I saw a spirit with an uncanny resemblance to my mother. Instantly drawn in its direction, I pulled away from Gabriel to get a closer look. When I did, my heart leapt for joy.

I stared at my mother's smiling face as we hovered there among glowing walls of the cybrary while streaming code sped past us. I couldn't believe that she was here after having felt what I did those few days before Ella passed away. I quickly learned that when it comes to discovering truths about the other side, you must be willing to let go of all preconceived notions as well as any bits of knowledge you think may be accurate.

"Mom, I thought you were reborn."

"I was."

"And um, now you're here? Did I miss something?"

"You missed a lot," she grinned and then took on her glowing form in the shape of an orb. "The part you recognize as your mother is but one particle of what I am, Chantel." She illustrated this as one of her tendrils drifted past me, leaving a trail of glowing dust.

"I am everywhere and yet nowhere." She was speaking softly to my mind now. "I was reborn in China and in America and in places you probably haven't seen yet or know of. And yet I am here with you."

"One particle?" My eyes were fixed on a single speck of dust still drifting before me.

"One particle, Chantel. I am the Source of what you know as your mother, and yet even my entire form is but one particle of the ultimate Source of Creation, from where we all come and to where we must return."

So, where is this Source and how do we find it?

Return to the Origin of All Things

Upon waking up from the dream, as many on the other side call it (some even call it a game), you are kept in close company with the angels—your parent angel and those that may have served as your mentoring angels during your lifetime. As you acclimate to being home again, you undergo a two-part review.

The first review is given by the Council, a group of twelve heavenly bodies of light that grade you not on what you did during your lifetime, but on how much you learned. It's here that each moment of your life is held under a microscope to see how well you performed the tasks you initially set out to do. There is no pass or fail with this review. It's merely another phase of the learning process for the human soul.

During this review, your parent angel remains by your side. He's a mediator, of sorts, that explains to you anything you may not understand and helps keep you grounded. After all, you just got back from the equivalent of a journey to the moon and here twelve reporters are asking you all kinds of questions as you review footage of your life. You haven't even gotten used to the gravity shifts yet, much less to the fact that you just died and are waiting to be sent to Heaven ... or to Hell.

Archangel Uriel revealed to me that it never fails—nearly everyone standing before the Council is shaking in their boots, wondering if they're going to get assigned a pair of wings and a cushy white cloud, or assigned to shoveling coals in the infernal realms.

According to the archangels, you don't get either.

Because our lives are already scripted, we've done away with the notion of free will in the human world. God already knows what's going to happen and how you'll react to it before you're even born, so to sit you down and judge you for a long list of sins that even *you* knew you would commit before you left Heaven is pointless. The only sin here is not learning the life lessons through the challenges written for you, and the penalty for that is having to do those challenges, or something similar to them, all over again. That's not to say that you have to relive the life you just left, but you will have to write into your next life script the challenges that will help your soul learn and evolve to the next level.

Then there are those who don't have much to review because they weren't in the human realm very long to begin with. These are souls that enter the realm only to leave while still very young. Such humans are highly evolved and are close to becoming, if they are not already, spirit guides. They fully understand that their purpose is to help teach others by making an early departure. Because of the immense pain often felt by those left behind, the souls return as spirit guides to offer comfort, encouragement, and guidance.

After the first review is completed, you are then accompanied by your parent angel to a place where you feel comfortable. It is there where you two have a heart-to-heart talk. This second review is highly informal, and depending on the angel, you could get anything from, "I knew you could do it!" to "I warned you! Didn't I warn you? I so totally warned you." But it's all lighthearted and good-natured. The point is to ease you into remembering who you truly are—not a human with flaws, allergies, poor social skills, and a bum knee, but a beautiful, radiant child of God who just enjoys playing masquerade... a lot.

Depending on the life you chose, during this time with your angel, you may meet up with loved ones. But those who have chosen darker paths for the purpose of fulfilling God's Great Equation will need time, *a lot more* time, to acclimate.

The Notion of Hell

It seems to bring some people comfort to believe that those who hurt them, or those who have committed heinous crimes against humanity, have a special place reserved in Hell where the offenders will be eternally tormented for their sins. But the truth of the matter is, the ex-husband who refuses to pay child support, the cyber thief who cleaned out your bank account, and even the serial killer prowling along the interstate all have a part in the divine plan.

Nothing—absolutely nothing—can happen in this reality without the Source's approval.

When I've discussed this with clients, I've had some scoff and call me crazy. Some have pushed away from the table in disgust with, "I don't want to go to Heaven, then, if so-and-so is there." I've even had clients get up and walk out on me.

No, I don't want to think that I'm going to wind up in the same place as those who couldn't do right by me in this lifetime. And I definitely don't want to go somewhere where murderers and rapists get an automatic get-out-of-jail-free card. The thought turns my stomach, yet I've seen those people beside the very same people we might consider saints on the other side. But I wouldn't have known this unless I had been told. In the Realm of Spirit, we drop the human form for the most part and instead take on our true forms of pulsing orbs of light—all connected by a silver thread, or umbilical cord, through which we communicate and interact.

But the souls who carry out such nefarious deeds don't come back to the Realm of Spirit with a clear conscience. Remember what I said earlier about how we all take back with us the emotions and memories of the life we just experienced. For the majority of us, it'll be difficult enough to forgive our sixth-grade teacher for humiliating us in class or our boss for cheating us out of four hours' pay. But for those who have gone through much darker lives, there is a quarantine period, a cleansing period of sorts where they are not allowed to rejoin the populace upon return.

I should also note here that this quarantine is not enforced to protect the good and kind people of the afterlife, but to protect those who were the embodiment of some of humanity's worst nightmares.

When a soul awakens from the dream and brings back the horrors they committed in a lifetime, it is much more difficult for them to accept the spirit world than it is for others. The guilt is so intense and oppressive that a soul can't shake it off immediately and is thus sent to a place under the watchful eye of archangels who are delegated the task of helping those souls to remember who they truly are.

Some souls bounce back fairly quickly.

Many do not.

So this notion of Hell that weaves in and out of history and cultures is not a place where souls go after having been judged. It's where they go when they can't stop judging themselves.

While on a tour of Heaven with Archangel Gabriel, we were in human form and I was with him in a very busy metropolis that looks like something that would have made Gene Roddenberry faint with awe. As the angel guided me through the dense crowd, I saw two angels flanking a man who looked drawn and a bit unkempt. His complexion was grayish, his eyes were sunken, and in the midst of all the other incredibly happy souls, he stood out. The man walked slowly as he kept his head bowed low between his shoulders, almost chin to chest. There was an air of shame and hopeless resignation about him. It seemed as if he didn't want to be seen, but the two angels flanking him held him gently by each arm and were encouraging him to look up, to look around.

"What is this?" I whispered to Gabriel as I stopped to examine the trio. Others who passed them by didn't seem to notice. But many stopped to hug the man tightly or to pat him on the shoulder and offer words of encouragement. Despite the welcoming citizens, he didn't seem affected. The dark cloud that hovered over him seemed oppressive.

"He's being reacclimated. The angels are showing him where he's supposed to be and that he's welcomed, not scorned." Gabriel responded quietly as he stood next to me.

"Why would he be scorned? This is Heaven."

"He isn't being scorned. He simply *believes* that he is."

I looked up to the angel in confusion. "How is it someone can be unhappy in Heaven?"

Gabriel sighed heavily and glanced at his feet for a moment as I saw a wave of sadness flash across his cherub-like features. Then suddenly he spoke: "Follow me."

In an instant we were somewhere that to this day still sends chills up my spine. Up until that moment, I'd only seen glimpses of Heaven, both the metropolis where the majority of people walk about in human form, and the metropolis where the majority of people move about in their spiritual forms. So far, everything I'd seen had been breathtakingly beautiful. Flawless. And there are no words to describe how incredibly awe-inspiring the Source itself is. But where we were now was the complete opposite of that.

We stood on a rocky cliff and looked across a dull, gray valley. There were dark storm clouds rolling overhead. Lightning streaked the sky and thunder shook the ground. Gabriel pointed in the distance, and I followed his gaze only to gasp at what I saw. I knew instantly at whom he was pointing.

Lucifer.

"Are we in Hell?" My voice shook as my fingers clutched Gabriel's robes.

"No, though many would call it that."

Gabriel went on to explain to me that this was the place where souls that weren't ready to rejoin the main population came. Burdened with grief, guilt, anger, or vengeance—among other things—souls meandered about in tattered clothing. They cried out and tore at their hair. They even fought each other, but to my shock, angels intervened. It was then that I realized there were no demons here, no grotesque, disfigured remnants of what used to be angels. And Lucifer...

Lucifer is Archangel Michael's twin. But you could definitely tell the difference in their demeanor. Archangel Michael was bright, always smiling, always playing around and offering words of encouragement. This twin stood upon a cliff in dark, menacing armor with his arms folded and a scowl on his face.

"He's not tormenting anyone?" I whispered to Gabriel.

"That's not his job. These souls torment themselves. He is merely the keeper of this place." Gabriel spoke without the disdain I imagined an archangel would have for the one who allegedly betrayed God. Key word here: "allegedly."

It turns out that Michael and Lucifer are twin brothers, the firstborn of the Source, with two very different views of the human soul. Michael believes in humanity and that the human soul can evolve with the right nurturing. Lucifer found the human soul to be corrupt and wanted the first of them to return to the Source. In other words, he wanted them destroyed. There was no huge battle in Heaven. No one defected. At most there were philosophical debates until one young angel came along who would fight for the human souls to remain a part of Heaven. You can read about him in appendix B.

Every angel has his delegated task, and since Lucifer has little to no love for humans, he was appointed to the realm where the most tormented of souls go until they heal. And that's why there were angels there, not demons. The angels walk among the souls to soothe them and try to help them remember who they are. In essence, these souls came out of their human reality carrying with them great burdens that keep them *feeling* human, that keep them stuck in their dreams. All in all, these are the sleepwalkers, and with tender nurturing, patience, and care, they will eventually awaken and return to the main populace.

So how does Lucifer fit into the whole world of arch-angels? He doesn't. He wanted nothing to do with humans and had no desire to interact with them in their dreams and illusions. And so here he remains in this purgatory of sorts, watching with a keen eye and allowing no one to leave until he feels they can rejoin the citizenry of Heaven.

If that's the case, then why is he, Satan, and the Devil so feared and so dominant in religion? Well, we humans bring with us some subconscious memories from the spiritual world, and the world of torment is associated with the energy signature of Lucifer. It's our way of trying to remind ourselves to let go of our hate, guilt, and other destructive emotions before we go home. For if we fail to do so, that's where we wind up. Not because we sinned—because sin doesn't exist—

but because of the feelings we may carry over for having committed a perceived sin or some heinous act that was part of God's plan from the very beginning.

In my first book, *Azrael Loves Chocolate, Michael's A Jock,* I wrote that Archangel Uriel has to be one ticked-off archangel to have been demoted to fallen angel by some monk at one point. But now, I sort of see why that monk may have done that. Uriel has little love for human souls as well, but it wasn't until I saw Lucifer that I realized Uriel must at least have a little hope for us. After all, he's an archangel that's sent to walk by our side, even as he longs for Armageddon. And he is also a very capable teacher, although a bit harsh. The point is, Uriel is at least approachable by human souls. Lucifer, however, is an angel we'd just best avoid. He's in a perpetually foul mood and wants as little to do with the human soul as possible.

Now at this point, some of you may wonder if Judas or Hitler is there trying to avoid the angel's icy glare. Perhaps Nero and Torquemada are sharing a cave somewhere near.

Historical figures that have embodied unfathomable darkness and caused near cataclysmic destruction, the likes of Hitler, were never the incarnation of human souls to begin with. There are beings who are appointed such tasks because no human soul would ever be able to carry out such despicable deeds.

It Always Comes Down to God's Great Equation

So, is this to say that Hitler was written into God's Plan? As much as it galls me to say it, yes. And so was slavery, oppression of the Native Americans, the bombing of Hiroshima and Nagasaki, and the destruction of the World Trade Center.

It's all or nothing here. Either God is all-powerful and all-knowing and thus sees everything that is to come in this reality, or he isn't and human life is completely left up to chance.

I choose to believe in a God that is all-powerful and all-knowing.

Some may say that God is cruel for besetting upon humanity such nightmares. To that I wag my finger and say, "Not true." We knew before we came here what we were stepping into. My African ancestors knew before they were born the struggle that slavery would bring to them. My Cherokee and Blackfoot ancestors knew that their unblemished lands would be stolen. My French ancestors knew they would have to endure one of the bloodiest revolutions in human history. Everyone knows upon the crafting of their life script just exactly what is going to happen to them: what they'll be born into, what challenges they must endure, what crises they must survive, and how they will ultimately depart this life— or, as they say in Heaven, wake up from the dream.

I must be emphatic when I say that we as human souls know and understand the peace and perfection that is the Realm of Spirit, which is why we're not fazed when we walk into disasters like the Great Flood, the bubonic plague, and even Armageddon.

We know, even if our avatars don't.

And this is what vexes many of the angels.

Archangel Michael told me that you can always tell when a world is about to be deleted and rebooted, as it were. He said that the population for that realm increases exponentially because everyone wants tickets to the huge event.

"Everyone gathers to watch the fireworks," the usually jovial angel chuckled tensely. "It just makes our jobs as archangels even more difficult. We don't enjoy watching the destruction of a realm, and we certainly don't enjoy being the harbingers of it. No matter how many times a world is destroyed and rebuilt, it's never easy."

Perhaps the Master General is speaking only for himself and a few other angels. There is one angel I'm aware of, however, that is so stoked for Armageddon, I'm surprised he's not standing before the Throne of God every hour going, "Is it now, Lord? How about now? Now? Soon, though, right?"

That would be the angel of the Apocalypse, Archangel Uriel. God creates a world; Uriel goes in with a flame thrower and shuts down the entire operation once it's run its course. And for an archangel whose purpose is also to guide us humans, he does his demolition job with an eerie sense of relish. I know from firsthand experience that Uriel really has little hope in the evolution of the human soul, but he does have hope nonetheless—more than Lucifer. If he didn't, he wouldn't be standing over my shoulder right now. Granted, he's coiling his fiery whip over a tight fist and muttering, "Any day now," but should any of us require his keen wisdom or profound philosophical tutelage, he won't balk at the request.

To Uriel's glee, yes, the day will come. This world will end and we'll all be on the other side, clambering over each other to see what new and exciting world God has given us to play with. Like actors in a television drama, there are the good guys, the bad guys, and the poor schmucks that get caught in the crossfire. But once the cameras stop rolling and the lights shut down, we can all put our arms around each other, smile, and flip a coin for who's going to spring for dinner afterwards.

We're more than just flesh, bone, and blood. Like our Creator, we are eternal and glorious beings. There is no end to us. There is no end to what can be our eternal happiness. Sure, there are those intermittent moments when we decide to enter a human world for kicks, but in the grander scheme of it all, we know we're just playing pretend. We're like children hopping from one ride to the next at an amusement park. Some rides are cheery and fun, while others put so much fear into you, you're praying to God the entire time. But once your feet are back on solid ground and you look back at that big, scary ride, you realize it wasn't that bad. In fact, you could take it on again and not wet your pants this time.

This is the practice we receive as human souls. These are the lessons we endure in a quest for the supreme understanding of who we are as children of the Creator and siblings of his most beloved archangels.

chapter five

CONTINUING THE JOURNEY

It's July 2012 and the Midwest is caught in a brutal heat wave. As I sit here praying the city's power holds up against the millions of air-conditioning units running overtime, I can't help but think back on the days spent in that dark, cluttered room that would reach 103 degrees even if it was only 80 degrees outside. Even if I ventured out of the room to sit in the claustrophobic hallway, the humidity would still have me clutching for dear life to my asthma inhaler and wondering if my congestive heart failure would finally decide to take me away from the hell that was that house.

The memories are still fresh. The wounds are still seeping.

About two years prior, even after I had published two books, I had come to the conclusion that I couldn't take anymore. With the failing economy, the only place I could take this broken body was onto the streets. I'd been on housing lists for years. I'd contacted every charity in Michigan, charities around the country, even charities outside the United States. I spoke to every social worker imaginable, and they just continued to transfer me to departments that were of no use or to phone numbers no longer in service.

The truth was I was stuck without friends or family, penniless and disabled, with only a computer and a will to write and somehow help others from slipping through the same cracks I had. Still, there was a part of me that felt that regardless of whatever spin anyone puts on the state of our country, or the state of the world as a whole, and no matter what a person's religious or political affiliation is, no one cares about the poor and suffering. And if they care, they don't have the answers. And if they have the answers, they don't have the wherewithal to bring to fruition their ideas. Of course, there are exceptions to that rule, but I feel they are few and far between.

For me, options had run out. I was tired of being in constant pain. I was tired of eating food that I knew was killing me. (I'd finally saved up enough to buy an electric skillet so I could at least eat hot meals, but they were all cheap, processed foods loaded with fat and sodium and God knows what else.) I was tired of being confined to my upstairs prison, of not seeing the moon or the stars, of not feeling a cool summer breeze or smelling the autumn rain. I was tired of knowing that if I died, it'd take about a week before anyone realized it, even though there was someone always in the house.

But then I kept saying to myself, "You could be in a shelter. You could be on the streets." For years, I kept saying this situation was better than the streets. At least most days I was safe where I was.

I was treading water in a sea of hopelessness. Yet all the while, I was reaching out to others online, trying to give them hope, trying to help them to hang on even as I felt my own fingers slowly slipping from the rope that had kept me from drowning during the last seven years.

"Uriel," I glowered at the ceiling one night after another day of unmitigated physical and emotional agony. "You've got until January 1 …"

"To do what, exactly?" The archangel appeared with his features pinched, his eyes piercing.

"I've suffered enough. I've lost everything and everyone. You angels got your damn books. I'm done. Either make some waves by January 1 or …"

Before I could finish my sentence, the angel flashed from the opposite corner of the room and appeared so close to me that I could feel the heat pouring off him.

With gritted teeth, he put his finger in my face and spoke slowly, "Don't you ever … ever … give me, or any other angel, an ultimatum like that."

Unmoved by his rage, I shrugged. What was he going to do, kill me? I'd been praying and begging for death anyway!

"I just gave it to you," I said without blinking. Uriel took a breath to speak, but then Archangel Michael appeared in a burst of white light. The Master General and I weren't on speaking terms and hadn't been for a while after I told him earlier in the year that he could go to Hell … if it existed. I had grown weary of constantly hearing, "Hold on, Chantel. Just a little while longer, Chantel." He was starting to sound like a broken record. All the angels were, and I was sick of it.

I had reached my breaking point.

When Michael appeared, I put up my hand before he could speak. "There is nothing you can say that will change my mind about this." Neither angel responded even though it felt as if we all were holding a collective breath. Uriel, who was my mentoring angel at the time, looked as if he wanted to throw me through a wall.

Without a word, the two angels suddenly vanished, and it was that moment that fortified my resolve. I knew what to do. I knew what was to come. January 1 would come and I would finally be free of this pain, either by my hands or theirs. I didn't care which.

As summer slipped into autumn and autumn into the many festive holidays, all of which I spent alone and in silence, a sense of peace eased over me. I knew freedom was just around the corner, and I counted down to the new year with more happiness and zeal than I had in all the previous years combined.

With the dawn of 2011, Heaven had remained silent. So be it.

I began writing letters to those few who still mattered in my life, as well as to some of my readers. It was only then that I began to feel lower than ever. I realized that I was a fraud, after all. I'd published two books commissioned by the archangels—the messengers of God—themselves, books that expounded upon their benevolence and compassion and the importance of hope, wisdom, and love. Yet here I was about to commit an act that went against everything I had penned. I was about to take my own life.

But what do you care if people talk? You'll be dead and happy, I selfishly tried to convince myself. I slowly looked up to the e-mails I had written, swallowed hard, steeled my nerves, and refused to change course. But just when I was about to click send on the first e-mail...

My computer crashed.

The three-year-old laptop didn't freeze or even blue-screen. It simply flickered and shut down. I tried desperately to reboot the system, but I could only get it to function in safe mode.

"What the hell is this?" I fought with the piece of junk for hours. In all my years of being glued to a computer, I had never seen anything like it. It would boot up, flicker, and then shut down again.

In the midst of my trying everything to resolve the issue, Archangel Uriel appeared with his arms folded and his stony gaze pinned on me. "Problem?"

At that point, I knew I'd just gotten checked by the angel of Armageddon while playing a most dangerous game of real-life chess. I was livid, to say the least, but I ignored him as I tried to at least get online in safe mode. My modem had barely been working before the crash, and now getting to my e-mail was proving to be near impossible. Not to mention, I had written the letters in the e-mail application, an antiquated piece of software that didn't save drafts. Hence, all the letters that I'd poured my heart, soul, and pain into had been obliterated with the simple flicker of a screen.

In a rage, I bellowed and cursed at Uriel. He knew me better than I did. I was too much of a perfectionist to simply bow out without a few eloquent lines to express the reasoning behind such a cowardly and weak-willed decision. Hot damn, I was pissed, and when I looked up at the angel as my system crashed for the fifth time in an hour, I wanted to throttle him. As if responding to the silent barbs I was spitting at him through my glare, he got into my face again with his finger pointed. Normally I would have been too pissed to balk, but something in his gaze this time sent a chill over me, and I couldn't quite figure out what it was. It shook the very marrow of my bones, and I even inched back a bit upon the bed where I was sitting.

"Don't you ever threaten me like that again, do you understand me?" he spoke in a low, steely tone. I tried to hold on to my bravado against the fiery angel as I challenged him to a blinking contest.

"Do. You. Understand. Me?" It was a harsh, rugged whisper. "Woman, you had better make that your first and last time you ever speak to me like that. If you do it again, you will lose more than a stupid computer."

I couldn't help the ice dripping from my tone when I responded, "I've been praying for death for years. I offered my life, and you refused to take it."

The angel growled low in his throat, and that's when Archangel Michael appeared again.

"Uriel, go," the Master General said simply. But Uriel and I had our gazes locked, and I think the only thing that might have separated us would have been a bucket of ice cold water. Even then, I was doubtful. He wasn't moving and neither was I, even though angry, frustrated tears were now cascading down my cheeks.

"Petulant…" Uriel breathed.

"That's an order, soldier." Michael's tone was a lot sterner this time, and the red-headed angel disappeared. "Chantel," the General sighed, "I'm going to tell you this one time and one time only. You cannot threaten us, coerce us, or try to twist our arms to do your bidding." His tone was unlike anything I'd heard from him before. Normally Michael was all smiles, but not tonight. He stood in my room like one would expect of an army general—as if he meant business. "After all we've done for you. After all we've shown you..."

"Michael, I'm tired!"

"I know," he said, nodding. "But you'll have to wait a little longer."

At that point, I couldn't contain my emotions. "Oh, just fuck off!" I threw a bottle of medication in his direction, and with that, he was gone. I could have thrown a few more bottles at him. After all, I was on fourteen different medications at the time. Instead, I lay down, drew my hands wearily over my face, and wept myself to sleep.

The next day, I was on the phone with technical support only to find out that the company that sold me their name-brand computer had the worst customer service in the world. After spending hours on the phone with them, I was told it would take about two weeks before a technician could come out and repair my system.

No big problem, I thought. I had my BlackBerry. It had been given to me as a gift when my computer had started encountering issues picking up wi-fi signals a year prior. I had been using the phone as a backup modem.

"I'll show them [angels]," I whispered, still determined to go ahead as planned. All I needed was to program my e-mail account info into my phone and voilà, I'd be back on track.

Or not.

Just as I set about my task, I noticed that my phone wasn't getting a signal. I then used my emergency backup cell to call the person responsible for the phone bill only to get a recording: "This line is currently experiencing trouble." Well, that was obvious. Both of our phones were on the same account. I then called the person's home phone.

"Babe, I'm sorry, but I lost my job. I didn't want to tell you or worry you, but I ran into some issues and there is no way I can pay the bill right now. I'll get it paid in about ten days."

Checkmate.

After hanging up, all I could do was fall back onto the bed and laugh. "I really hate you," I grumbled heavenward at the angels. I had thought I was bored and miserable before, but without the ability to get on the Net—my only connection to the outside world since I only left the house every six to eight weeks—I realized my wretched life could get a lot worse. My computer would only work for about ten minutes at a time before it would crash, so I made Facebook posts when I could, trying to be a cheerleader and beacon of hope for everyone else when in fact I myself was falling completely apart.

"Now that I have your undivided attention…" I heard a voice. I knew that voice all too well, and I wanted to run and hide just to get away from it. That, of course, would have been a move made in vain, because when Jesus wants you, he will find you.

I was in deep trouble and I knew it. Michael, the snitch, had run back and…

Who am I kidding? Jesus knew I had been giving Uriel and Michael hell all year anyhow. My spiritual father had been calling my name, asking me to visit him in meditation, but I pretended not to hear him. I pretended that I was too occupied with research and writing books to talk.

Well, without the computer, I could do neither, so it was just me and him without any distractions of the Internet or text messages.

I could cop an attitude with my brothers, the archangels, and get away with it, but I dared not even make eye contact with my father. In fact, I sat with my head bowed, fearing that I was about to see a side of Jesus that I didn't want to think even existed: his angry side.

But I was wrong. Jesus, in his infinite wisdom and compassion, hardly looked perturbed. His voice was calm and even as always as he reviewed with me the challenges I had faced during the seven years of hell in what I considered solitary confinement—my own personal Guantanamo Bay.

There had been so many harrowing moments during those years that I lost count, but I walked through each year with Jesus and saw the challenges—financial, medical, social, mental, emotional, and spiritual. And then I saw how the angels had guided me through each and every one. I likened the experience to walking through a dangerous, untamed jungle with a guide walking ahead of me to clear the path with a machete. I was still snagged by a few thorns, was slapped in the face by an occasional tree branch, and even bitten or stung by annoying insects. That is to say, each experience kicked my butt one way or another.

Yet, I'm still here.

I remember back in 2008 when my routine blood results from a doctor visit placed me on a temporary quarantine. My white blood cell count had plummeted so low that my doctor initially feared I might have been stricken with leukemia.

I was told not to leave the house and to stay out of public places and avoid anyone who had anything contagious.

With a compromised immune system, even the common cold posed a serious threat.

And all of this emerged just weeks after the debut of my first book, *Azrael Loves Chocolate, Michael's A Jock*.

I sat in my room in total silence for hours. I remembered back to when doctors had thought I had leukemia when I was seven years old and I'd had the exact same symptoms: low white blood cell count as well as low platelets. To this day, I can still hear my own screams as the doctors performed a bone marrow test.

I wasn't about to go through that pain again. And I felt I shouldn't have to.

"I did what you said, Lord. The angels told me to write a book. You got the book, and this is what I get in return?" I was incensed. It wasn't fair! While drowning in hopelessness, poverty, and emotional anguish, I had still managed to attain my biggest dream of becoming a published author. And now, it seemed that I'd have little time to celebrate the accomplishment, as death would soon be knocking on my door.

After the rant I directed heavenward, Archangel Raphael appeared with his hands gently folded before him.

"It's not leukemia, Chantel. Please, do not tax yourself with worry and fear."

"But the doctor said ..."

"Chantel, trust. It's not leukemia. I promise you." With that, the angel was gone. Still, I worried, albeit not as much. I would, over the course of two months, follow up with more blood tests, and to my doctor's astonishment, they came back normal. Somewhat, at least. Granted, there were other issues that had to be addressed, but I was wholly against the treatment for them.

"You do realize that without treatment, you're setting yourself up for all kinds of health complications in the future," my doctor said, agitated by my obstinacy. I knew the risks of my condition, and if an early death were to be the result of it, so be it. In my view, the treatment posed more risks than the illness itself, so I was determined to find alternatives. It would take me four years to find that alternative, but once I did, my condition improved and treatment was no longer required. It's a condition that can creep up at any time, but at least when it does, I know what to do about it.

And that point brings me full circle. When I had the stroke in 2004, the doctors were baffled and informed me that they couldn't find the cause. Sure, I was a big gal—though much smaller than I am now. Since the stroke, I've gained quite a bit of weight from doing nothing but sitting in a single room for seven years and eating cold ravioli out of a can. But back then, I was a vegetarian. I went to the gym three times a week. Yet I was frustrated, because I had been diabetic since the age of twenty-two, and here I was nearly thirty and still trying to get off the medications used to treat the condition.

In early 2003, I had gone to speak with my doctor at the time to get referrals to a nutritionist and nephrologist. But instead of giving me the referrals I requested, my doctor had insisted that I take a third medication, a new medication that had shown remarkable results with his patients. With a sigh, I had accepted the prescription, grateful that I had insurance because otherwise it would have cost me over two hundred dollars a month.

Eighteen months later, I was in the hospital, paralyzed by a stroke that no doctor could find a cause for.

One late night in 2005, I had come down out of my upstairs prison to take out the trash. The lady of the house was a night owl and was watching television. Just as I was about to make the painful trek back up the flight of stairs to my room, I overheard a commercial.

"Have you or a loved one recently suffered a stroke or heart attack? Were you or a loved one taking _____," the same medication that my doctor had prescribed for me back in 2003. Yes, in fact, I was still taking it!

"You could be eligible to join a class action suit …," the commercial continued.

The next day, I was on the phone.

By October 2010, the suit had been settled, but I was one of about two hundred other cases that the pharmaceutical company had rejected. This knowledge was what contributed to the deep depression that had caused me to threaten Uriel. I saw no way out of my plight. I had no money, no assets, no family, and no friends who could help.

I had come to the conclusion that I was going to die in that room, but damn it, it would be by my own hands and on my own terms.

After Jesus had shown me the good that had come out of my being there—being in a safe shelter and having time to commit to writing while exploring my spirituality—I calmed down a bit. But what really veered me off the road of self-destruction that night was the person, or being, that had accompanied Jesus during our talk. I'd seen this being before, and for the longest time, I thought he was a new archangel being introduced to me. But as he and I talked over the course of 2010, I came to realize that his energies were nothing like an archangel's. That, and he had an aura that I had seen around other beings that had been visiting me ever since 2008.

I simply called this being "Bo." It was the first name that popped into my head, and to this day, he has yet to correct me on it. After our discussion and review of those difficult years, Jesus left me in Bo's capable hands, and that's when 2011 really started rocking.

Immediately, we got to work.

With my computer working in safe mode, I opened up Notepad and took down Bo's dictation word for word. His first order was to begin cleaning and start throwing out anything I didn't need, want, or hadn't used in the last seven years. After that, I was to begin packing. He revealed to me that I would be moving very soon, but I would have to do so quickly and silently. I was to tell no one of my plans, and I was to keep the details of the move, as well as my future whereabouts, to myself. The latter part frightened me. After all, why did the whole thing sound like some covert, black-ops strategy? Why would I have to be so secretive about it?

Well, as I mentioned earlier in the book, we cannot escape the laws of causality. And as I would soon find out, the tipping of one domino would eventually leave me no choice other than to follow Bo's chilling instructions.

Still disgruntled and skeptical at the time, I gave him the same response I usually gave the archangels: "If you say so. I'll believe it when I see it."

It would take about two months, not two weeks as promised, for the incompetent electronics company to repair my computer. But while it was down, service returned to my BlackBerry and I began making calls to every housing and apartment complex within a hundred-mile radius.

Unfortunately, as I had encountered over the previous seven years, there was nowhere to go. The economy in Michigan had sunk faster than the *Titanic*, and entire families were vying for more economical housing as foreclosures spread across the state faster than a flu epidemic.

But then the first hot day of the year came in early April. My room hit 90 degrees. At that point, I was moved into action. I ordered boxes from U-Haul and began packing. I didn't have anywhere to go and no money to travel, but I refused to endure another year of hell in that room. If I had to put my things in storage and wander the country for a while, I knew I had to mentally and emotionally prepare myself to cope with it.

Before that, however, I thought I'd try an organization for disabled people just one more time. I had called them before over the years only to be forwarded to other centers or charities that didn't have the capacity to help or had guidelines that I didn't qualify for.

This time, I finally got through to a caseworker. I told her about my situation. I told her about my health conditions and the risks of living another summer in a 103-degree bedroom without air or proper ventilation, in addition to no access to the kitchen or laundry.

The worker seemed angry at the homeowners, but I insisted that they weren't at fault. They were letting me live there and leaving me to do my own thing without taking rent money. Though I had paid them quite a bit in the past, they had refused to accept more funds from me. It was something I couldn't understand, really. I just assumed it was out of generosity and maybe they really did care to an extent.

That's when my newfound caseworker angrily chimed in, "No, Chantel. If they take your money, that makes you a tenant and makes them official landlords who would be responsible for providing safe and adequate shelter." I could hear the rage and indignation in her voice. But more than that, I could hear her passion. "Think about it. If a fire breaks out, you have to get down those stairs and out the door…"

My heart skipped a beat. I hadn't thought of it before in those terms. At the bottom of the stairs was the front entrance with a security door that could only be opened with a key that I didn't have quick access to. Although I knew where the keys usually hung in the kitchen, even after seven years I always struggled to remember which key unlocked the front door. I did have a key to the garage door, but if a fire broke out in the kitchen, that pathway would be blocked. And as cluttered as the house was, it would take less than four minutes before it filled with dense, black smoke only to hit flashpoint seconds later. Moving at the speed of a three-legged turtle, it would take me five times that long to get down the stairs, much less out the door, for which I first would have to scramble to find a key.

Furthermore, because I had never rented before, I didn't know the laws. I thought the homeowners were just trying their best to be tolerant and charitable. Then again, they knew of my health conditions and knew that extreme heat was a serious health hazard.

"I'm calling Adult Protective Services [APS] so they can get you out," my caseworker huffed, and I could hear her rattling papers.

"No!" I screamed. "You'll only make things worse. In seven years, I've only had one friend visit me inside this house. I didn't even get physical therapy because I couldn't help the feeling that somehow it'd be an imposition." I was shaking so badly, I could barely hold the phone. "If you send APS, these people will kick me out and I have nowhere to go!"

But there was nothing I could do. In my caseworker's eyes, I was in imminent, life-threatening danger, and by law, she was required to report it.

After we hung up, I was so sick with worry, I couldn't keep any food down. I didn't sleep. I stayed up for twenty-four hours waiting for the death knell that would be a visit from APS.

The agent arrived around ten AM, and instantly I knew my life was about to end when the man of the house came up to angrily bang on my door and demand I come downstairs. I had wanted to talk to the agent in private and clarify the situation for her. In no way was I trying to implicate the owners of the house.

The agent questioned me as the man of the house sat there, angry, red-faced, and with bulging eyes that looked as if they were about to pop out of his bulbous head at any moment. As a cold, intolerant, and reticent person, he rarely had a kind word to share with me, but that day he was chattier than a teenager during lunch period, leaving me no room to respond to any questions the agent was asking me. Finally, after a moment of listening to his answers, she turned and abruptly interrupted him.

"I'm talking to *Chantel*. Do you mind, sir?"

That only made him hotter, but his wife called him out of the room, and it was then that I broke down into silent sobs.

"You have to help me, please. But first, let me explain everything," I mouthed silently, knowing that our conversation could be easily heard in the next room of the small home. "Come upstairs," I whispered. I wanted her to see and feel what I had to endure.

"He won't allow it," she whispered back as she gestured to the other room with a quick tilt of her head. Sick over the whole confrontation, I sat down. I'm unable to stand for long periods of time, and the heat along with a sleepless night had worn me down to nothing.

"Chantel," she patted me on the shoulder, "I can see you're a bright and intelligent woman. Given that you have your full faculties, there is nothing I can do for you."

"Then why did you even come here?"

"Because I was informed that you were in some type of danger."

"I am," I silently mouthed back at her. "If you'd just come upstairs…"

"Chantel, do you believe in God?"

The question caught me off guard. This woman was a government employee, not a nun! What did that question have to do with anything we were talking about?

Nevertheless, I answered, "With all my heart and soul."

"Then pray He delivers you from this. It's rather simple," she chuckled and turned for the door.

I couldn't hide my anger and disdain for her flippant attitude and said, "You'll have to forgive me if I don't walk you out." I gestured at my body with a graceful flourish of my hand. "As you can plainly see, my mobility is quite limited."

As I look back on that moment, I realize how arrogant and pompous my actions were.

"I understand," she said with a shrug and then pointed at me with a smile. "Keep praying." With that, she stepped out the door still chuckling. She was laughing at me. Laughing!

Never before had I felt such rage flow through me. I knew what she was thinking, but she was dead wrong. I was a productive citizen. I paid taxes. I gave to charities. I had a college education and two published books under my belt. Damn her, I was not the worthless wretch that she thought I was.

I couldn't hold the emotions in any longer. I had been holding them in for seven agonizing years. As I slowly made it back up the stairs to that hellish oven, I bellowed so loud, I think the entire neighborhood heard me. I'd had enough of being treated like trash.

Now more than ever, I was determined to get out.

But now, it was a matter of getting out before I was kicked out. No doubt the homeowners were thinking I had called APS on them, and that was not the case. All in all, the situation was one big clusterfuck, and I knew the clock was ticking.

I called my caseworker and told her what had transpired. I was right—her calling APS had only made matters worse. She then promised she'd help me get out, but I knew she was simply placating me.

Sure enough, she forwarded to me the same numbers that everyone else had in the past.

The truth is, there is little to no help out there. I felt it then and I still feel that if you're poor, you're unheard and unseen, which makes me wonder why all these organizations even exist. (That's a rhetorical question, really. Of course, I believe most of these organizations, but certainly not all, exist to pad their own pockets.) I mean, why did my caseworker even have a job if she was so ineffectual at serving the very people her organization claimed to serve?

At the end of the day, I encourage anyone stricken with similar circumstances that befell me to fight. Don't give up. I didn't give up. I refused to be unheard and unseen, and that determination—fueled by burning indignation—is what moved me into action.

At that point, I knew I had to muster up strength I didn't feel I had. After a day of packing, I searched for housing. The places where I could afford the rent were either full or in areas far too dangerous for a single, disabled female to live.

As boxes began to stack up in the upstairs hallway, and I was loading the curb every week with ten thirty-gallon bags of junk I no longer wanted, the man of the house approached me one morning at six o'clock as I dragged bags out the door.

"So when are you moving?"

"I don't know," I said dryly.

"That's not the answer I want to hear."

"Well, that's the only answer I have for you, sir. When I find out, you'll be the first to know."

I went to every apartment search site I could find, but something on my search sidebar caught my eye one night. It was a link to a site I hadn't thought of, and to be honest, it was a site that didn't have the best of reputations. Still, I was compelled to take a look.

Less than a week later, I was touring my first apartment. The landlady seemed kind, but sassy as well. She showed me the small apartment, and as I looked around, I began to weep.

The building was old but well kept. Still, because of its age, a lot of the fixtures were identical to those that I had grown up with in the family home, from the ceiling light globes to the ceiling fans to the marble window sills—sills that I used to fall asleep on as a child after a night of star and moon gazing. Basically, the apartment was a miniature version of the home I had grown up in.

Without hesitation, I told the landlady that I'd take it and agreed to move in within the week. Her daughter was with her, and I told them that I was a loner and kept quiet and to myself. I also told them I was looking for something permanent. I honestly didn't have the health, strength, or wherewithal to move again any time soon.

"You're the exact tenant we're looking for. The previous tenant lived here for thirty years until she had to move into a nursing home. If you want to stay here that long, you're more than welcome … just so long as you stick to the rules," the landlady said, squeezing my arm as I dabbed at my tears.

I left knowing that within seven days, my life would begin anew. Bo had been right! He had been too accurate, actually, because four days later, I received a text from the son of my soon-to-be former landlords. It was an outrageous, irrational rant full of false accusations, but then again, I wasn't surprised. I had, after all, lived with the family for seven years and knew them all too well. I knew the accusations were a cover for the anger over the APS visit, though he vehemently denied it. But I hadn't talked to any of the family since that dreadful day, so the sudden explosion of indignation and contrived drama was to be expected. I simply kept my cool through it all.

"The sooner you're gone, the better," his text came through.

I chuckled. In three days I'd be gone. I had borrowed money so I could make a reservation with the movers, and the packing was nearly finished. It was as if a boss were telling me I was fired after I had already told him I quit.

"Give me thirty days," I pleaded on the text message. First, I wanted leeway in case something went awry. Second, I was following Bo's instruction: leave quickly and silently. Three days later, the movers showed up and cleared me out in less than an hour. Without a word, I gave the man of the house the key to the garage door and didn't look back. While en route to my new home, I called the phone company to have my phone number changed immediately, thus cutting off any form of communication with the family. Before I arrived at my new place, I had my new phone number. With a sigh of relief, I declared that this chapter of my life was finally closed.

When I moved in, I had no furniture save for a lawn chair, a TV tray table for that damn laptop, and a table that my friend Britt had given me when she closed the tea shop. I didn't even have a bed, but I did have a camping cot built for large folks that was actually comfy.

A year passed and I sat there staring at boxes I couldn't unpack because I had no furniture in which to store my things. Frustrated, I called the law firm handling the class action suit against the pharmaceutical, and they said they still couldn't prove my case. Though I was enraged on the inside, I calmly asked them what more proof they needed. Blessedly, it was a simple document that I had come across while packing. I knew exactly which box it was in.

I faxed it to them.

Upon receiving that one simple piece of paper, the plaintiffs approved my case. The win was bittersweet, though. This corporation had ruined my life, left me permanently disabled and penniless, and all I received for sitting in a dark room for seven years wasn't even enough to buy a new compact car.

But it was enough to buy a desk, a new computer, and basically everything I would need to turn the apartment into a functional office. I didn't buy a sofa, cushy chairs, end tables, or a television. I've no plans to ever entertain here. Normality for me is an office setting. It always has been since I first worked in one when I was thirteen.

Seven years of misery.

Seven years of solitude.

Seven years of fighting "the system."

Seven years of enduring something that had the potential to kill me at any moment.

Yet, I'm still here.

The angels never left me. They brought me through, and now I've begun a whole new adventure. I'm excited. I'm motivated.

But most of all, I'm validated. Without the angels, I would not have made it through the darkest, most painful chapter of my life. Without the angels, this book would never have been written.

And on that note, I'd like to end here with one final point.

Less is more. The 2,400-square-foot family house is gone. I don't own a car. In fact, I publicly made a vow of poverty. I no longer have the typical American disease of "gotta have," nor do I desire to live a life beyond my means. Life is much simpler now, simpler than I ever thought it could be. Bills are paid, healthier foods are in a kitchen that I actually have access to, a kitchen that is clean and honored as I was taught it should be—as the hearth and heart of the home.

Unlike what a few clients have said to me, I'm not writing books for the money. Frankly, I've told people in lectures and consultations that if they want to become a writer, don't quit their day job.

At the end of this particular hardship, I've learned humility, patience, compassion, and self-love. And so I've written this to help others understand why life challenges are presented to them and how they can navigate those challenges with the help of divine assistance, even if they're as pigheadedly stubborn and self-pitying as I used to be.

I realize now that the journey for me is far from over. There will always be challenges, uphill battles, and rickety bridges to cross, but as I look back at my ordeal and see how the angels carried me through it all, even with my kicking and screaming, I know that they'll carry me through all my future trials as well. The only difference is I'll let them do so without having to deal with any dissent, disbelief, or disrespect.

The archangels are very real. Heaven is very real. The only proof I can offer you is my life story. But better than that, if you just reach out to the angels and embrace them as your cosmic brothers and sisters, you'll have all the proof you'll ever need. Your life will become the evidence that proves that not only do they exist, but they also serve as the guides our souls need to navigate this human experience.

Brightest blessings on your journey. I sincerely wish you well.

appendix a

JAKE'S STORY

For years I had been curious about the passing of Jake, my spirit guide, but it seemed I was too selfishly caught up in my own personal drama to be interested in the life he had once lived not so long ago. At our initial meeting, I had asked for him to provide proof of his identity and asked for clues to his existence that only a chosen few would know. Most importantly, I asked for clues that could be validated. To my disappointment, he provided nothing more than a simple response of, "It matters not what I did in the past. What is important is what I'm doing right now."

Well, what Jake was doing in the "now" was putting up with my constant complaining and lack of faith. But before he had to endure his current assignment of building my confidence as a medium so that other angels and guides might connect with me, he first had to deal with passing through the veil between the human world and the Realm of Spirit.

I found it odd that I had never asked Jake what it felt like to die. Not in all of the sixteen years we'd been together had the question ever crossed my mind, so it came as a huge surprise when he decided to write this chapter and relay to us all the shock and frustration he encountered when he was suddenly taken from this existence in his mid-twenties.

While at first I was stunned to learn that Jake's transition to the other side involved some personal turbulence, I now deeply appreciate his candor. I know beyond all doubt that his personal account of his encounter with sudden death and progression to the Realm of Spirit will teach us all valuable lessons not just to recall during our final hour, but to meditate upon while we still breathe.

In Jake's Words

The night I departed the human world seems more like a fading bad dream. I barely remember it now, and I fight to recall the details.

I was at work hammering away on a major project that night. It was late, or early, depending on how you look at it. The night didn't seem too much out of the ordinary—a lot of waiting on my part, waiting for other people to finish their jobs so I could finish mine. I was mentally exhausted. The work day had been twelve hours too long, but it was work that was almost done. A few more days and I could go home, finally. I'd been away too long from my family and the people I loved.

The waiting was finally over and it was time for me to work. I knew what I was supposed to do, but then something went wrong—horribly wrong.

I didn't feel anything at first except that my breath was taken from me and I couldn't inhale fast enough. I fell to the floor; I heard voices, and everything went dark almost instantly. When I opened my eyes, I saw people scurrying about. I heard screams. I stood up and followed the chaos to see what was going on, and I saw myself lying there on the floor. Stunned, I gazed in disbelief. Trembling, I tried talking to someone next to me. I then began screaming at everyone, but no one heard me.

"Oh my God! What happened?" I heard a coworker scream.

"What the fuck just happened?" screamed another. I stood there, frozen in terror. It was then that I felt a hand on my shoulder. I whipped around to see a man robed in white. His dark hair curtained down over his shoulders, and I had to crane my head up to look into his somber eyes. He didn't speak; he only stared at me.

"What is this? What's going on?" I demanded of him. My emotions were a turbulent sea of anger and fear, and the man's silence only increased my fear a hundredfold. "Oh no. C'mon, not like this! NOT LIKE THIS! NOT NOW!" I bellowed in rage.

The robed figure turned and walked away from me, past the chaos and through a door that stood in the middle of the room, a door bathed in bright blue light. Frustrated, I turned back to the chaos to watch my body being rushed out of the room. I tried to follow, but I couldn't. Instead, I was compelled to turn toward the blue door and walk toward it.

"What, no goodbyes? No last words? Nothing?!" I stood in a room that was dimly lit with an ethereal blue light that seemed to come from nowhere. There were now four men standing before me. The tallest one, the one I had followed, spoke first.

"There's no need, Jake. Everyone knows how much you love them." He sat, though I didn't see any chairs around. He just casually levitated before me.

"Who are you?" I wanted to scream at them, but what good would it have done? I realized where I was, sort of. More concisely, I realized where I wasn't—among the living.

"I am Raphael. This is Michael and Gabriel. And this is Cassiel."

"Angels. You gotta be shittin' me," I groaned as I rubbed my eyes.

"More humans say that these days," Raphael commented to Gabriel, who shrugged and looked at me as if he were amused by my crude reaction.

"I told you, no one believes. Good thing we don't get bent out of shape about it," Gabriel said as he approached me. I took a few steps back, now knowing how a mouse in a lab cage feels. Gabriel circled me a few times and looked me over. It was then that I realized I was completely naked. You go back the way you came in, I guess.

"Okay, so what now? I'm not a Christian." Why I was compelled to say that, I have no idea, but it seemed that Gabriel was only more amused by my confession.

"Funny, neither are we," he chuckled. Gabriel stood before me, but he was not nearly as tall as Raphael or as bulky as Michael. He was lean, with the face of a cherub, and his head was crowned with blonde curls. His sapphire eyes seemed to look through me, as if he were reading my mind, reading my heart, my soul.

"I don't get it." I looked to the four angels but directed my comment to the quieter one, Cassiel. There was something about him that frightened me and intrigued me at the same time. He hadn't looked at me once, or at least not that I'd noticed, but my eyes were fixed on him as I silently willed him to look my way. When he did, a chill came over me and I was overcome with tears.

"Ironic, isn't it?" he spoke softly. I was taken aback at how much we resembled each other. I walked to him and gazed into what looked like my own eyes. He offered a soft smile and then glanced at Michael, Raphael, and Gabriel.

"I'll take it from here," Cassiel muttered, and before I could follow his gaze, the other three angels were already walking away.

"I'm not a Christian." Michael seemed to mock me.

"Well, more and more humans are saying that," Gabriel sighed, and they were gone.

"Am I going to Hell?" Memories started crashing down upon me, memories of good deeds and not-so-good deeds. What really tugged at me were thoughts of my mother, my sister, and my fiancée. Would I ever see them again? There were so many things I wanted to tell them, to tell my friends. There was so much left undone.

"Do you want to go to Hell? I can arrange it," Cassiel said off-handedly as if it were a common request from the dead. I felt as if my heart had dropped into my stomach, and the feeling must have translated to my eyes. Cassiel put up his hands to calm me. "Chill, man. You're not going to Hell."

I simply shook my head and was somewhat relieved that it was an option I could pass on. Without another word, Cassiel walked away. Naturally, I followed him with my mind full of questions to which I could not lend my voice. We walked for what seemed like forever in complete darkness. I could see him just fine, and myself, but there was nothing around us except this silent void.

After a long while, I finally asked, "Where are we going?"

"You tell me. You have questions. I'm just walking until you say something."

"Can I see my father?" The thought hit me suddenly. I had not seen my father in twenty years. He died when I was a child, but his legacy had haunted me well into my adulthood. He was an artist in his own right, the likes of which your reality may never see again, and as a highly respected professional, he had throngs of students whose interest in his skills had brought immense attention not only to his art but to his charismatic personality. He quickly became a legend not only in my mind, but in the minds of many—a legend that is still honored to this very day. But at the pinnacle of his career, he made a quiet exit from the human world, leaving behind his students, friends, and family. And me.

I grew up in the shadow of his legacy, desperately trying to avoid it and live up to it at the same time. So many nights I had cursed his existence, raised my fist up to the sky in anger and spite, demanding answers: I wanted to make a life that was my own, but I carried his last name, his eyes, and obviously a part of his soul. He was inescapable it seemed. No matter where I went, I was never me; I was always "his son." So what better time than now to ask him why? Was it something I had done or something he had done? Upon his death I was left with so many questions, knowing that only in my own death would I get answers.

That moment was upon me now, and I couldn't stop shaking with anticipation.

"Jake, there's no sense in asking why." Cassiel had watched me process dozens of questions and even more emotions in the matter of a nanosecond.

"Well, *why*?" I prodded. This was my chance to get all the answers I had waited a lifetime for.

Cassiel turned away, rolling his eyes in supreme annoyance. He led me to a door in the darkness and placed his hand upon it.

"Because everything just is, Jake. And the only answer you will ever get, but that will never satisfy your human mind, is 'because.'"

"You sound like my mom when she used to say, 'Because I said so,'" I grumbled.

Cassiel opened the door, and we both were bathed in sunlight.

"Um, how about some clothes, or does everyone run around Heaven naked?" I had been covering myself with my hands up until that point.

Cassiel shoved me through the door. I whipped around to look back at him, but found myself instead staring into a lush forest. With a huff, I looked down at myself to see that I was dressed Cassiel-style with a pair of black jeans and a t-shirt.

"Thanks, I think." I looked up to the bright blue skies and then made another one-eighty to face a magnificent garden that brought back countless childhood memories. I was home. Though I couldn't remember if the garden had really been home at one time or just a childhood dream, I know that I always felt at peace there, safe.

Wind chimes sang on the breeze as I wandered down a winding brick path toward a crystal-blue lake. I stood on the shore, taking in the grandeur of the moment. I felt compelled to kneel before the majestic mountains across the lake as I watched them reach into the cloudless infinity of a sun-kissed sky, but then my eyes drifted upshore to a bamboo bridge and curiosity carried me there.

The bridge stretched across the lake to a gazebo that floated effortlessly on the waters. And then I saw him. I stood in silence, though with some amusement, and watched him; I remembered him being so much taller when he was alive. Perhaps I was no exception to those who always thought my father was larger than life.

"What took you so long?" He smiled but never interrupted his meditation.

"Had to grow up, I guess, and finish what you started," I smirked as I sat on the floor and watched him like I used to when I was a kid.

"Ah, all the *trouble* I started, you mean. Mother still angry with me?"

"No, she loves you, Dad. You know that."

"You still angry?"

"You've no idea." My heart sunk. The word "why" was on the tip of my tongue, but I held it there thinking of Cassiel's warning.

"I was finished. It's just that simple, son."

"Just that simple? Dad, you left us there alone. It's like you were there and then you just suddenly disappeared into thin air like Houdini. And to make my life worse, everyone starting looking at me as if you would suddenly reappear through me like some phantom. Like somehow I would be able to resurrect you or reincarnate as you ... *become* you. I knew that at the funeral. Everyone was whispering as I walked by and I pretended not to hear, but I did hear them, Dad. Maybe I imagined a lot of it or embellished the memories a bit, but I know what I felt. I remember feeling that I had to be you now 'cause that's what everyone wanted. That's what Mom wanted."

"It's unfortunate that you felt that way. I only wanted you to be whomever you wanted to be. That's all."

"Well, you weren't there to tell me that, now were you?" My words were biting now, and I was back on my feet. The anger I had kept inside for twenty long years had finally come to the surface at full velocity, and I paced near the door of the gazebo wanting to hit something—anything!

"Then hit me," Dad simply said, and I turned to him, my eyes full of shock.

"What?"

"You heard me. Let me see if you learned anything worth learning." My own father, the man I had come to revere and respect with my whole soul, was taunting me to a fight like some street bully.

The challenge diffused my anger and brought a sly grin to my lips. I circled my father, sizing him up. Yeah, it was time to show him how far I had come without him.

I took my place before him and bowed deeply. I held it, realizing what was happening. It was the moment of a thousand lifetimes. I was really here! I was with my father again, but in a flash it dawned on me that he hadn't aged a bit. He was the same as I remembered when I was a child, so I couldn't help but stare a while. Like the lake around us, his eyes reflected sunlight at me as he smiled. He must have known what I was thinking: I was planning to take it easy on my old man, but he looked to be in better shape than I was.

"And we're waiting for … what?" he taunted. With that I made the first move, and in the warmth of the sunlight, in one of Heaven's many gardens, we sparred like two tangling dragons. It was like a dream; maybe it was a dream. But do the dead dream? Or do they live their dreams? At the moment, I didn't care. More importantly, I didn't care enough to ever ask why or how. I just know that for that moment, I experienced a joy that no words could ever express, even though my father, in all his strength and grace, royally kicked my ass.

"My son, you have my heart and my will, but you still need a lot of practice." With that he walked away, across the bridge, and disappeared inside a little cabin. I just stared at him with my mouth wide open, surprised for a few moments, before I followed him into the cabin.

He placed two bowls on the table. "Sit. You have a long journey ahead of you." With that, it was as if he had ripped my heart out for the second time.

"What?" I said, leaning over the table and gazing at him. "I just got here. Why do I have to leave?"

"Because you're not done. You have a lot more work to do, son."

"And you are done? You're just retiring like that? Dad, talk to me. I don't understand any of this!" I quickly took his hand in mine. "I don't want to go."

"You have to. We all do. We all have work to do, son."

"What about you? Where are you going?"

"Same place as you … eventually."

"Dad, no riddles. C'mon." In case you're wondering, you can get headaches in Heaven, and I remember mine being massive. Maybe I just imagined it, but I distinctly remember rubbing my temples and then my sinuses. Great, I was allergic to the flowers in Heaven's garden and was beginning to understand why some people may have asked Cassiel to direct them to Hell after all. Heaven didn't offer answers, just more questions!

"It is not a riddle, son. I told you before, it's simple. Stop making things complicated."

"Wha ... complicated? We haven't even *said* anything yet!" My head dropped to the table in defeat with a thud. "Just send me to Hell," I moaned.

"Be careful what you ask for ..."

"Yeah, yeah," I groaned again. I got up and went to the window to look out at the lake again. Surreal doesn't even begin to describe the sheer beauty of this place. The sun was setting and the stars were already high in the sky. The scene was magical.

"Mom's gonna kill both of us," I smirked. My father sighed with me and put his hand on my shoulder.

"I've no doubt of it, son. No doubt in that woman whatsoever."

"So is it like this all the time here? Is each day always so perfect?" I peered out the window, and still there was not a single cloud in the dusky sky.

"It can be if you want. It only rains here when you want it to." My dad patted my shoulder and retreated to the fireplace.

I could easily say that I stayed a lifetime there on the lake with my father, playing catch-up for the years lost between us. When he said that I had to leave on a journey soon, I feared leaving but quickly came to the realization that I had to cherish the time I did have with him. When I took that understanding into my soul, time stopped. The sun stood still, and night never came.

By the fireplace, my father and I talked forever, it seemed. And you know what? I was so caught up in his life and he in mine that the question *why?* never came to mind again.

Just when you begin to get settled in and come to the realization that Heaven is as good as it gets, there comes a knock on the door. I had no idea how much time had passed before Cassiel came along to yank me from my paradise, but he looked oddly out of place in the sunlit garden with his pale features, dark eyes, and raven-black hair. In stark contrast to Raphael and Gabriel, he wasn't the happiest or prissiest of angels, to say the least.

The dark angel pushed his way past me and into the cabin, surveying the room like a recon soldier. He found my father sitting in the corner with his eyes closed, meditating.

"He's going to hate you, Cassiel." My father's lips didn't even seem to move.

"He won't be the first one," Cassiel said, bowing deeply to my father, who simply nodded back.

"Hey, don't talk about me like I'm not here. What's going on?" And my father was right. I would hate Cassiel, as the dark-winged angel turned to me and handed me a piece of paper. It looked like a rolled sheet of legal paper, but when I opened it, the damn scroll fell to my feet, hit the floor, and rolled out the door and into the garden.

"What the hell is this?"

"Unfinished business," Cassiel said as he sat at the dining table and began eating *my* lunch. No, I was not liking him at all. "That's everything you've got to complete before you go back."

"Go back? I'm not going back. I'm happy here!" I was scrolling through what looked like Santa Claus's checklist from Hell. It was names, nothing but names.

"I told you," my father said with a bit of amusement in his voice. "He's stubborn, like me."

"Like you used to be," Cassiel corrected and then approached me. "Vacation's over. You've got work to do, but first a debriefing."

"What the fuh ... ? You're joking, right? Dad, tell me he's joking."

"If it were Michael, I would say yes, he's joking, but ...," my father muttered matter-of-factly.

"I don't joke. I'm not known as the patron saint of jokes. You of all should know that," Cassiel fumed, and with that, we were no longer standing in my father's house but were back in that dark, silent vacuum. And damn it all, I was still holding my list of names.

"First you'll report to the Council. They'll assess what you've done. If you want to appeal the list here, that's your best chance to do it."

"Who are you, my defense lawyer?" Council? Council of whom?

"I've moved up a notch. Last time we were here, you called me the prosecutor."

"Last time?" I arched my brow and glared at him. What the hell was that supposed to mean? In that instant, his entire body flashed before me, nearly blinding me. I shielded my eyes for a moment until the light dimmed. I then looked up and beheld a radiant golden light. It was formless and constantly changing, with luminous tendrils, leaving wisps of light as it ebbed and flowed. And strangely, I knew I had seen this before … several times before.

"I remember now," I exhaled and turned to look up into the darkness to see twelve other orbs of light. As memories came flooding back, I knew I had indeed been here before. It was then that I looked down at the long list and realized it was my handwriting. "Why didn't you talk me out of this the last time I was here?"

"We tried to," said a soft, feminine voice surrounding me. "We know that those born of Cassiel's energies tend to be the most obstinate of souls." Her voice seemed to smile.

"So many to tend to," I continued as I scrolled through the names on the paper and sighed.

"You have the time. Unless, of course, you'd rather not pursue the task at this time, Jake. You are free to do as you wish."

"No. No, I want to get as much done as I can. I'm promised to a few on here." I smiled a bit as a few familiar names rolled in front of my eyes: they were friends I had not met among the living but had known all too well from the Realm of Spirit.

I had my work cut out for me, there was no doubt of that. Keeping the promises made to those on my list would be easy, but much of the work relied on interrealm communication—direct communication between the human world and the higher realms. Establishing connections would prove a bit daunting. It seemed like eons since my contacts and I agreed that our life paths should merge on this level, but I remember telling them, "Don't worry. I'll think of something creative," when they asked how I would manage to get in touch with them from this side of the fence.

"We're not worried about you," my friends had said when we made the arrangements. "We're worried about us not believing in you." We all knew that passing through the veil into the human world was like being anesthetized, like going into a coma where we're completely closed off to the reality around us. In essence, we equated becoming human to slipping into a dream where we're at the mercy of our five senses. And because the brain is easily fooled and often appeased by what it experiences, rarely do we question whether or not the experience is real, whether or not it is just a dream.

Those who have engaged the sixth sense begin to see past the dream world and out into the higher realms in which the dream is contained. Contacts that had done this would make my job of establishing connections a lot easier, but still I held some pity for those who had chosen to open their spiritual eyes in a human lifetime. Now that I look back on the experience of my most recent life, I realize just how dumb I was. But that was the existence I chose, to sleepwalk through that life just for the sake of ease. Actually, at the expense of enraging philosophers and clerics ages old, I will even go so far as to say that being oblivious is not always a bad thing.

Am I saying ignorance is bliss? You bet. But just because I chose to live a life oblivious to my spiritual existence does not in any way imply that I left purposes undone. Quite the contrary. If my only purpose was to be oblivious so as to be an example to someone else of how not to live, then my deed was done. I came to this understanding after the Council dismissed me and I once again found myself following Cassiel in darkness.

"So, how did I score?"

"You tell me," Cassiel grunted. "Did you learn what you wanted? Did you experience what you wanted?"

I paused and instantly thought of the unfinished business I had left behind with those I loved so much. But that was business that the human side of me clung to. As I reflected back upon my intentions before I was even born as Jake, I realized that even my death, as well as what I thought was unfinished business, had all been part of the planned experience, part of my purpose. Cassiel continued walking, leaving me to process my thoughts, but then he returned to my side with a softer gaze in his eyes than what I had seen earlier.

"Did you accomplish what you went there to do? Think back on the last time you went to the Council and arranged all this. Did you finish or not?"

"Yes, I did." I had asked for certain experiences and gotten them, and after a moment of reviewing my life and my short twenty-something years, I finally resigned myself to what my father had said: I was finished. It was just that simple. Well, I was finished with that part of my existence anyhow.

Since receiving my itinerary, I have been steadily working with my assignments—those I am to connect with. I know now that I am a child of Cassiel, the angel of tears, forged of his strength and spirit to help bring balance to those I encounter. While serving as a guardian and confidant, I have observed a flood of tears, pain, and injustices. So my work is never really done. I am still quite busy helping those I am promised to, but I have all of eternity to do it, for what seems like a lifetime on Earth is but a simple exhale and inhale in the Realm of Spirit.

Chantel asked me years ago if I missed the family I left behind. While it is painful to watch them grieve, I see them every day with the understanding that grief is a part of their learning, a part of the experience they chose for this lifetime. My family may not realize I'm still with them, but they don't need to. I didn't realize that my father was watching over me during the twenty years we were apart, and yes, there were days when I felt lost and alone without his presence in my life. I know now that my father never once left me, as I will never leave the ones I love; it's impossible, for everything in this universe is connected.

In the end, I take comfort in knowing that the connections we share with those we love are reinforced by love and are impervious to time, space, and death. Then again, I contradict myself. There is no time, no space, and no death, but just a thin veil between worlds—places where time stands still, places where souls are intertwined and connected, places where death is a passing whim, a fading notion for those who once lay asleep but are now awakened to the vast and spectacular beauty of a universe without end.

GABRIEL'S STORY: THE UNSEEN PASSION OF THE CHRIST

I had never seen [Archangel] Michael as incensed as he was the day all the angels had been called together for an announcement of colossal proportions. No one was sure what was about to transpire, and even I—a minister of communication—was out of the loop. But when I saw my brother Michael emerge from the throngs of us who were there, I felt fear, and that is not an emotion that we angels experience often, if at all.

With a grim look on his face scolding enough to send an entire world of humans scrambling for cover, he stood tall with a wide stance in his human form and announced with a resounding, commanding voice that one of us was entering a human reality.

Initially, I did not believe such an announcement was cause for alarm because we angels weave in and out of human realities all the time. Contrary to popular belief, many of us have had very human experiences, some of which were assignments that human souls were too young and inexperienced to achieve—and not all the assignments were what many humans would consider to be of "noble" purpose, but they were of divine purpose, as you'll soon find out.

What made this moment so significant was that one of us was going to fully immerse himself into a human reality. Now, allow me to clarify that I'm using genders here for ease of your understanding. In Heaven, all of us—including you—may appear as one gender or another, but in our true, spiritual forms, we are genderless. There is nothing in our spirit form that would make us male or female. This is what makes us perfect beings, because we are in perfect balance, carrying within us the potentialities of all gender traits. Moving on…

The feat of completely immersing oneself into a human reality had not been attempted before. In fact, I know of no angel who had even pondered the notion, and I personally didn't see a need for such an effort. Though many of you envision us angels in human form, like yourselves, we angels—being the firstborn of the Source and the first of individual consciousness—are pure, uncorrupted energy. Speaking in simple terms, we possess the ability to shed particles that are capable of becoming another angel entirely. (This is the exact same way souls are born of the Source.) The shedding of these particles does not deplete us, yet allows us to be in many places at the same time.

We're everywhere, and nowhere. We can cross the illusion of space-time without moving. For instance, if I were to shed one million particles of my being, they would become one million Gabriels that were all of the same mind and connected to me, the Gabriel-Source. Hence, even as I relay this information to you, I'm engaged in countless experiences. Humans have this same capability, though not on as grand of a scale. You're still children in terms of spiritual maturity, our baby siblings whom we love, nurture, and hope will one day be as elevated in knowledge and wisdom as we are.

Despite being capable of sending just *one* particle into the human realm to fulfill whatever divine will the Source decrees—which is what we angels tend to do—Archangel Michael had announced that one of us was, as you humans put it, "going all in." It had not been done before. And quite frankly, the thought sent a collective chill through all of us.

When Michael announced which of us was to make this attempt, there was a silence that seemed to last an eternity. If we'd been in physical form, I'm sure I would have felt my heart drop into my stomach, for it was revealed that the most evolved of us, the most cherished, was going in. This is the one who embodies the energy that your current reality recognizes as Jesus of Nazareth.

Because of this, it was then all too apparent to me why Michael looked so grim.

Jesus, for as high as his status and power rank, is still younger than Michael. Michael and Lucifer were the first of the Heavenly Hosts to emerge from the Source—twins, whose consciousnesses were very much alike...until human souls emerged from the Source. Upon the emergence of human souls, there were those of us who looked at our siblings as simply another—albeit strange—facet of the collective consciousness. But then there were those, like Lucifer, who saw the humans as flawed. They were spheres of energy that were easily corrupted, imbalanced, and lacking in their connection to, and even reverence of, the Source.

Jesus was not of that opinion. His wisdom far surpassed that of Michael and Lucifer, though he was not the first of us to emerge from the Source. Actually, he emerged as a separate consciousness some time later, but here in Heaven we tend not to take such things into account, for we are all born of the Source, of the Eternal Light that has neither a beginning nor end. There was no race to see who would emerge first. It just so happened that one individual consciousness developed and more followed thereafter. The order in which it happened is usually irrelevant to us.

But on this day, it was very relevant to Michael, for he saw Jesus as his younger brother. Michael does not boast about being the eldest for ego's sake, but instead sees himself as responsible for all of us as his "younger" siblings. He was one of the first, and hence feels it is his duty to watch over every single soul that comes into creation—angelic, human, or other. Despite being a "younger" sibling, Jesus possessed a power and wisdom that none of us had yet attained, not even Michael, and so in this, the eldest deferred to the youngest.

"Is there any way I can talk you out of this?" I heard Michael whisper to Jesus. Calmly, the young lord shook his head and placed his hand on Michael's shoulder.

"I have to know. I must experience what so many others are experiencing. Fully experience it," Jesus responded. I pondered those words for a moment because none of us had experienced imperfection. It was a last frontier in Heaven.

To have our entire being submerged in the human experience, to be completely human, was foreign to us. Because we're all interconnected, I heard the thoughts of many other angels mingled with my own: *What will happen? What if he doesn't return the same? What if he returns … corrupted? Then what?* We were wholly unprepared, but because the Source did not disagree with the young lord's desire, we had no choice but to acquiesce and follow his lead.

Michael glanced away with indecision playing across his face even as we all remained silent. To see the Master General of the angelic armies toiling over an internal war was unprecedented. To see him of the same mind as Lucifer, who felt the entire operation was a waste and a folly, was even more unnerving.

Because Lucifer was of the opinion that the humans and their lust for adventure simply didn't belong in the realm of perfection, Jesus then turned to him and said, "Your disdain for the humans will make you perfect for this challenge. You in your angelic form shall challenge me in my human form." There was a collective gasp, but Lucifer didn't so much as blink. The angel of light simply folded his arms and nodded.

"As you wish it, brother. I will show you no mercy."

I saw Michael bristle at his twin brother's display of power.

"I'm not asking you to," Jesus stated simply and then turned to the rest of us to disseminate the basics of what was to transpire in his lifetime and what his intended goals were. The human world that he was to enter hadn't even been created yet, which sent Archangels Raguel and Ramiel—assistant creators of human realities and their corresponding timelines—scrambling to create the chain of events that would lead to Jesus's arrival.

Countless other realities had been created … and destroyed. Such is the nature of Source to teach and nurture the human soul while accommodating the human soul's unending curiosity and hunger for adventure. But this reality that Jesus was to experience was one of the harshest yet developed. It had challenges set up within it that would push the human soul to its limits, and that, coupled with Lucifer's determination to see this experiment fail and thus garner even more support for his argument that human souls should be done away with, made the human reality even more harrowing. Still, this type of reality was something that many of us angels quickly aligned with because at the time, the human soul—which is a much smaller sphere (particle of the Source) with less energy, a smaller capacity, and a slower ability to process information—was evolving at a snail's pace.

This is not to say the human soul isn't perfect; you simply learn differently than we angels do, and your growth isn't as accelerated. Don't fret over it. That's why you have us—to help you grow. And that's why these current realities exist. With lessons learned through harsher experiences, human souls began evolving at a much faster rate. So the reality created as the stage for the story of Jesus was done so to provide one of the most challenging human experiences ever encountered. He already had an advantage because he was fully immersing his divine body, and because of that, the Source agreed to an experience that would push his spiritual power, and not just his human capabilities, to the limit.

Once the game plan was set in motion, we all knew our parts. We especially knew Michael's.

"There's no way I'm letting you go in there alone to face all of that and Lucifer's powers while you're at a human disadvantage. Don't even think it," I heard my brother say in a small effort to exert his status as eldest. Jesus, being understanding and loving as always, acquiesced, but only allowed Michael to watch over him from behind the veil, as many of you call it. Lucifer called foul on the move, but Jesus countered by noting that all humans are born with angels to walk by their side, angels that are only allowed to act according to divine will. Realizing the truth of that, Lucifer backed down.

Then there were the parts that yours truly played in this, though many of you know what those parts were. I was the one who had to tell a barely teenage girl that she was blessed to be pregnant... without having yet wed. But then again, the soul that you all know as Mother Mary had already stepped up and was the first to volunteer to be the mother of Jesus. And though she was a human soul, she did so proudly and eagerly. When word spread about this reality that was being created and what it all entailed—basically a showdown between Jesus and Lucifer—other human souls began flocking around the Source, requesting to be part of it.

But there were still so many parts of the puzzle missing, one being Mary Magdalene.

Determined to be by Jesus's side in any way he could, Archangel Michael drew Mary directly from the Source himself and imbued her with his loyalty, strength, and courage. Archangel

Iophiel blessed her with beauty, passion, and a fiery spirit that fueled my gift to her of speaking her heart and mind. Since Michael wasn't allowed to take physical form to protect and comfort Jesus, the Master General was sending the next best thing. And based on what we angels had learned of humans, men tended to feel even more empowered when they had supportive women around them. Still, considering the world in which Jesus was to exist, we had to tread lightly. The women would have enough challenges in and of themselves.

Coming from the other side of the polarity were the men—John the Baptist, the disciples, and the apostles—who were all chosen of human souls as well. And by God, did they all vie for those roles. Everyone wanted to play a part in this game, and all were doing their best to prove just how qualified their soul was for the job. Still, there were a couple of positions that no one applied for, but that were necessary in order to help Jesus fulfill his goals.

When the time came to seek the soul that would betray Jesus, no one would step up, not a human soul and definitely none angelic. Lucifer claimed he already had his hands full being himself.

And no one would step up for the role of Pontius Pilate, either.

At that point, Jesus personally appointed some of us angels for these roles, which Michael then called foul on.

"You won't let us protect you, but you would have us condemn you?" Michael argued, and I could see pain etched deep in his eyes that I'd never seen before. Doubt and uncertainty were emotions we angels simply couldn't understand. They weren't a part of our programming, but during this time, many of us would get a taste of them—not while engaged in a human experience, but while very much in our natural, perfect state. To say it was unnerving was an understatement.

"Purpose, brother," Jesus spoke in a near whisper. And there was great purpose indeed. With human souls progressing so painfully slowly, Lucifer had been pushing his agenda among other angels to rid Heaven of the humans. There had been some talk among us that perhaps all of them should be returned to the Source, reabsorbed, and done away with completely. We would all soon realize that by attempting to become fully human, Jesus was determined to prove that the human soul was not flawed, but merely different. After all, if the Source itself were perfect, how could something imperfect emerge from it? It was a philosophical debate we angels often engaged in. Some of us were curious to see how this new form of energy called a human would evolve, while others felt that allowing it to multiply would do nothing but cause problems, such as encourage us angels to take human form, to wear clothing, to eat, and to act without purpose and instead on impulse or whim—in other words, to play or do something simply because we desired to. Some even predicted that we angels would fall into total discord and break from the Source completely because of the "unevolved" humans.

Regardless of what many of you have been taught, that has not happened, nor shall it ever. The Source is all-encompassing. Its will is absolute. Though all of us in Heaven have free will, we are of the Source. We are of the singular consciousness that is in perfect balance. No one can go rogue. And there are some angels who believe that because of that, humans enjoy their realities, their dreams, where they can at least pretend and explore what it's like to step outside of their spiritual nature, to even go against it.

We angels, however, prefer our home close to the Source. We ourselves have evolved in countless ways, and Jesus himself was of the mind that the Source created human souls to further the wisdom of the angels, of the first sentient, self-aware beings. Could human souls be teaching tools for the sages? Jesus was willing to find out.

Still, Michael wasn't the least bit happy with the plan, in which betrayal and condemnation were paramount in Jesus fulfilling his purpose. For now, I cannot reveal to the masses exactly which angels played the roles of those who condemned Jesus to his death. I will say, however, that the human souls of Judas and Pilate, as well as the angels from whose energies the human souls were forged, still carry their burdens—in some capacity or another—to this very day.

For the longest time, no one knew which angels Jesus had chosen for the tasks. And it wasn't until long after Jesus had returned that the information was revealed. To this day, one might still see the haunted eyes of those who endured that experience, but Jesus is ever close to them. For some, the bulk of the burden has been cast aside. For one, however, his pain has become his armor, and he is now one of Jesus's closest confidants.

Journey of Christ

When the time actually came for Jesus to fully immerse and be born into a human world, Heaven was silent. The universe seemed to hold its breath. Mind you, we'd been preparing for what one might consider mere hours. Meanwhile, thousands of years had passed in the reality prepared for him.

I will never forget that moment. We had all taken human form. Michael and Jesus shook hands, though here, the gesture is more of grasping each other's forearm. It was a tight, firm shake, and I could see the torment in Michael's eyes. He didn't want to let go. None of us did. But we had to.

I had to head out right behind the young lord to announce his arrival to the humans who would find the child in a manger, while Raphael and Ramiel watched closely the planetary conjunction that would create the "star" heralding not only a new age in this particular human reality, but a new age in our universe. What was about to transpire was truly extraordinary.

When the young lord slipped into his dream and fully immersed himself into the human reality, there were no jubilant celebrations, there was no music. There was silence broken only by the sound of weeping. Our most beloved was leaving us. Leaving. And considering what we angels had to do in order to reorient human souls to the spirit world, none of us knew what to expect. We were all left guessing what Jesus would be like upon his return. And we were all hoping that Lucifer, with his acutely acerbic attitude toward this operation, would show just a little mercy. Knowing his disdain for humans, we knew it was a foolish thought.

You have to understand, we angels know a lot, but we don't know everything. We only know what the Source allows us to know, and because of the circumstances, though we were given a basic outline, we weren't given the full details.

Needless to say, the biggest outrage came at the crucifixion. Souls that stood by and watched from Heaven—both angelic and human—erupted into a thunderous outcry so loud that I was worried it would provoke a schism in the entire universe. And one of the bitterest, most heated battles I'd ever seen between two archangels was not between Michael and Lucifer, but between Michael and Cassiel. During Jesus's greatest suffering, Cassiel wanted to buffer him from the pain as much as possible. But Michael had his orders directly from the young lord: do not interfere.

All in all, the birth of Jesus into the human world was a great feat in ways humans could never imagine. And you've reason to celebrate, but if you think we angels were throwing a party, you're sadly mistaken. Many of us had very human moments of doubt and fear.

But among my many memories, what will always remain at the fore is Michael's resolve. He stayed by Jesus's side the entire time. As did I. Our lord was never alone. Not once.

———————————— ❦ ————————————

Many of you reading this have already experienced the time during the life of Jesus in this *current* reality. If you weren't there the first time, you went through the "simulation." Once a significant event or timeline in a reality takes place the first time, it is archived so other souls can experience it if and whenever they so wish.

I know what's truly going to vex you later is knowing if the reality you're in now is a part of the original timeline when Jesus lived, or if you're living in a reality based on a "simulation" of his life. Don't let it get to you. The point is, he was born, he lived, he died, he was resurrected in spirit, and he returned home whole and with even more understanding than what he left with. And considering he was the wisest of us to begin with, that says a lot.

After Jesus's return, it became mandatory angel training to experience human realities even more than we had been previously. We do it so we can continue to understand the human soul, because we still don't understand the whole attraction to drama, pain, and suffering, but we're trying to understand and to help you all one day evolve beyond your apparent need for these experiences as "entertainment" and especially as learning tools.

When Jesus returned, all of us had questions, but the young lord was weary and simply said with a soft smile and a chortle, "I'm not doing that again. Next time we'll have a different game plan."

Of course, Archangel Uriel is itching for that moment to arrive. The fiery angel of Armageddon is ready to control-alt-delete this reality or destroy it altogether. But as long as you humans seek to experience this reality, the Source will provide it. This reality will run its course, be "destroyed," and then be rebooted and ready for another run.

But no matter how many times this reality occurs, there will have been only one birth—one Christmas—which was in the spring, by the way, because that's Jesus's favorite season. But we knew the celebration would find its way into the winter. We won't split hairs on that one. You humans do enough of that without our help.

Because of Jesus's great accomplishment, humans carry the memory of him and his sacrifice in their spiritual DNA. It's not a Christian, Jewish, Muslim, or Buddhist thing. Remember,

Jesus isn't Christian. Technically, he's not Jewish, either. He is the King of Angels, a young angel himself who risked his very existence because he believed in the human spirit. Regardless of our religion in these realities, he is with us. He has many names and many avatars, and his story crosses religions in this world as well as others.

There are realities where Christianity, as you know it, emerged as a result of his "presence" in the timeline. There are realities where other, completely different religions emerge. That's why we angels repeatedly say that we have no religion. Our loyalty is to our king, the one of us who was the bravest, wisest, and most compassionate; to the one who didn't see the human soul as flawed, but rather as uncharted territory to be explored, understood, and nurtured. His act of complete selflessness and sacrifice saved the human soul in more ways than any one religion or doctrine ever could.

Jesus didn't do it for glory, nor to be worshipped, but to give the fledgling souls of the Source a chance to exist, grow, and evolve. In return, the only thing he asks for is that humans act with the same selflessness and treat each other with the same love and compassion so that they may learn from each other, as well as from the Hosts of Heaven.

—Archangel Gabriel

appendix c

THE ARCHANGELS

Here is a brief summary of the angels I've been working closely with over the past two decades. Some of them have already been mentioned throughout this book. If you've read my first two books, *Azrael Loves Chocolate, Michael's A Jock* or *The Angel Code*, then you're already familiar with these guys and gals, but I've added some new information that may prove incredibly useful when engaging them, so don't skip this section.

My new readers may be wondering why I only mention sixteen angels in this book and not an encyclopedia's worth. Well, I only write about the angels I interact with on a regular basis. When it comes to working with the divine, I use a method that I call "reverse angelneering." When an angel steps into my life, I avoid researching them as much as possible. I get to know them by talking with them and seeing how they move in and out of my life. I note what's going on in my world when they arrive, the wisdom they bestow, and how they approach various situations that arise. After a few months, I'll then research the angel to compare notes of my personal experiences with references ranging from religious and academic texts to experts in the theological, anthropological, metaphysical, and paranormal fields. This is how I validate the angel's presence, as well as my intuitive gifts.

But, there is a caveat. The angels will appear and interact with us in ways that we are receptive to; hence just because the angels appear to me in one way, it doesn't necessarily mean they will appear to you in the same fashion. When I first debuted as an author, I was adamant that I would not discuss what the angels looked like because I didn't want to impose my visions onto others. Well, that plan quickly folded because readers by the droves were falling just short of demanding that I describe these benevolent Hosts of Heaven. Hey, we're visual creatures, and so I was naive to try to dodge the topic. Eventually I dropped a clue here and there, and then I decided to show some artwork I had commissioned. It came as no surprise that I received two kinds of responses: "That's exactly how Michael appears to me!" or "Nah, I envisioned him differently."

And that's fine! The angels may change how they appear from one person to the next, but one thing is certain: they all have what I call an "energy signature," which means they have an aura about them that does not change. The summaries that follow offer icons, colors, numbers, and scents that resonate with each angel's energy signature to give you a better idea of how to recognize them. For example, Archangel Michael can appear as any race with any hair color and any accent, but we can all recognize the sun, the javelin, and the lion as his icons. And when we step outside on a bright, summer day to let the sun shine on our face, we feel the archangel's energy. We feel his presence—warm, golden, vibrant.

A word to the wise when embarking on this section: You'll see that I have listed ways to invoke the angel's energy for meditation or for mundane situations like taking an exam or celebrating a birthday. Note that I speak of invoking the angel's *energy*, not invoking the actual angel. Unlike so many other angel books on the market, I do not subscribe to having to conduct rites or even uttering prayers to entice an angel to stand by your side. Just call out the angel's name and know they will be there. I've lost count of the times I've been vexed by a situation and simply called out "Michael!" much like Aladdin called for his genie. (And yes, Michael has appeared to me with a comical look on his face and quoting Disney's version of the genie: "Poof! What do you need?")

Moreover, I definitely don't believe that silly incantations, candle spells, rubbing an enchanted lamp, or any other magic-related activity can persuade an angel to do your bidding—say, for instance, to get your boss to give you a promotion or to turn your crush's attention in your direction. The angels don't work for us, they work for the Source and the Source alone.

Now, I do believe that if you want to feel a bit more confident when you go into a job review for a possible promotion, you can invoke energies that resonate with an archangel's vibrations. That is to say, you can channel the angel's attributes when you need them. Some of you reading this may be old enough to remember the '90s Gatorade "Be Like

Mike" ad campaign. It was referring to the basketball legend Michael Jordan and implied that if you drank Gatorade, you could own the courts with masterful moves like Jordan did.

The same principle applies here. If you want to be like Mike, in this case Archangel Michael, then you can channel his vibrations of strength and courage by wearing his colors of gold, yellow, or white. You can wear a pendant of angel wings or a lion's head. You can even decorate your environment with bright images of the sun, sunlit oceans, and tropical settings. If you want to turn the head of someone you fancy, then invoke the energies of Archangel Sandalphon by wearing pink or light green. Send flowers or candy. Write love poetry.

Now, just as with drinking Gatorade, doing these things is not a guarantee that you will get what you desire, because I believe that no matter what we do, the outcomes in life are already plotted out. Nevertheless, invoking the energies of the angels helps us to better recognize their presence and better understand ourselves. You'll get to the point where you're so confident that you'll no longer feel you have to cling to a pendant with Michael's likeness. You'll feel so creative that you no longer feel you need a cherub ornament (Sandalphon) hanging from your computer monitor.

But let me warn you now that once you begin engaging the angels and getting to know them on a personal level, you will want them around "just because." You may feel that you don't need Uriel to take on a judge and a menacing traffic cop in court, but you will have become so close to him that he's the one you'll go to when you need to let off steam and vent about said cop. At this point you will have established a true and long-lasting relationship with your angelic brothers and sisters. You'll no longer go to them only when you want or need something, but just because you want to feel them close to you. That is, after all, the purpose of this book and the books before it: to help you get to the point where you see the angels as dear friends and family, not just as some supernatural beings that come to save you when you're in a bind.

So use this section to help familiarize yourself with your cosmic siblings. Get to know them so that one day you may be able to connect with them and bring more meaning to your life than you could ever imagine.

Archangel	Name Association
Ariel	Lion of God
Azrael	God Helps
Cassiel	Speed of God
Chamuel	Seeker of God
Gabriel	God Is My Strength
Haniel	Grace of God
Iophiel	Beauty of God
Metatron	Little YHWH (variant of Yahweh)
Michael	Who Is as God
Raguel	Friend of God
Ramiel	God's Mercy
Raphael	God Heals
Raziel	Secret of God
Sandalphon	Brother (Metatron's twin)
Uriel	Fire of God
Zadkiel	Righteousness of God

Archangel's Primary Associations and Duties
Angel of animal life, adventure, and discovery
Angel of death and transformation
Angel of tears; protector of the downtrodden
Angel of creation (nature) and balance
Angel of philosophy and communication
Angel of charity
Angel of the arts and celebration
Angel of the Akashic Records, libraries, and record keeping
Master General of the Archangel Armies; angel of warriors, protectors, sports, and competition
Angel of labor and community
Angel of research, history, and time
Angel of healing, astronomy, travel, and mysticism
Angel of secrets, mystery, metaphysics, and mathematics
Angel of love, music, academics, children, games & playfulness
Angel of prophets, visionaries, philosophers, and justice
Angel of saints, charity, places of worship, and the imprisoned

Ariel (Lion of God)

Come on, soldier, just a few more steps! You can make it.
To stop now would be the dumbest thing you've ever done.
And unlike my angelic brothers and sisters,
I will taunt you into eternity
if you give up just a few yards short of the finish line.

—ARCHANGEL ARIEL

Youthful and quick-witted, Archangel Ariel has a sharp tongue that most of her archangel brothers and sisters try to avoid, even the Master General, Michael. She's sassy and bold, and her no-nonsense approach to any dilemma can sometimes make her a bit too intense for even the shrewdest to handle. This archangel is the patron of all things related to the animal world, in addition to healers and those who protect the environment.

You can align yourself with Ariel's energies by focusing on one of her many icons, which include the lion's head and a medieval sword and shield. Her energies also can be found flowing through images of bears, hawks, cheetahs, and ravens, or through the scents of fresh apples, musk, pine, and even spicy pepper. Meditating in forests or open fields or near lakes can bring you closer to the angel's energies, especially on a windy day, as it's one of her elements, in addition to water.

Tuesday is Ariel's power day, as it best resonates with her energies. Her numerical vibration is three. You can invoke her attributes of courage, quick wit, and sharp intelligence with accessories of silver and pewter. Aventurine, crystal quartz, and emerald also harmonize with the angel, so keep them close to remind you of your own strengths and abilities to speak up for your cause.

Ariel particularly enjoys music that is full of passion and emotion, from the bagpipes to the flute, guitar, and banjo. She can listen to anything from soulful folk music to rock anthems—whatever brings people together in solidarity. And if you happen to catch the angel across the dance floor out the corner of your eye, you'll most likely catch her relaxing in loose denim—or cotton—in soft, muted earth tones accented with jewel tones.

Holidays that best resonate with Ariel: Easter, Fall Equinox, Friendship Day, Summer Solstice

Best times to channel Ariel's attributes: a sunny day at the beach; a day at an outdoor game; tailgating party; a relaxing day at the spa; backyard picnic; breakfast/brunch; when you want the courage to simply say hello or break the ice; when in love or flirting

> *You should always treasure your own uniqueness.*
> *It makes you cool … like me.*
>
> —ARCHANGEL ARIEL

Azrael (God Helps)

There will be times when you feel spiritually limited,
if not a bit stagnant.
This imposed moment of stillness
is necessary for you to learn restraint,
discipline, and how to accomplish goals
with minimal resources.
I understand such moments can be frustrating,
but these lessons must be understood before you can attain
your next spiritual level.

—ARCHANGEL AZRAEL

Contrary to what some may believe, Azrael, the angel of death and transition, evokes a great sense of peace and comfort whenever he draws near. There is never a reason to fear this angel, for he is one of the gentlest of God's creatures. But those who try to make his job difficult by clinging to this reality when it's their time to return to the Realm of Spirit may find themselves being unceremoniously carried away kicking and screaming. His main task is helping to make the transition from one life to another as painless and as smooth as possible, so he prefers that those he comes to collect greet him with a hug, instead of clinging to the bedpost and refusing his hand.

Azrael is the patron of death, the dying, and the dead. He watches over caretakers, morticians, and funeral home directors while lending support to those in the fields of hospice and grief counseling. Still, for an angel of death, he's quite an entertaining chatterbox, and those of you who engage him shouldn't be too surprised if you actually find yourself with an extra bounce in your step. Why would you engage the angel of death? Well, if you have a fear of death or you're having trouble dealing with the transition of a loved one—or even your own transition—what better angel to consult than Azrael? His presence is warm, loving, and compassionate. Oh, and he's a sucker for classic movies and Broadway musicals.

You can align yourself with Azrael's energies by focusing on his icons of the butterfly or raven. Images of the bat, beetle, and moth resonate with the angel's transient nature, while those of the crow, raven, and vulture serve as reminders of our mortality and how very fragile it is.

During my college years, my favorite place to meditate was the cemetery—the older, the better. At that age I had a profound fear of death, however. The fear was so crippling that it forced me to lose a year of college, as well as miss out on an invitation to study writing in Tuscany. I didn't know why the cemetery drew me in; it just did. To my utter confusion, it offered a sense of peace that I couldn't even find in my own home.

As I look back, I realize that I had been surrounding myself with Archangel Azrael's energies for security against my own fears. And they weren't just of death. I didn't like change, either. A transition of any kind often sent me into an emotional tailspin, but some transitions weren't as bad as others. I always welcomed new friends. I always found getting to know people to be an exciting adventure. So shifts in friendship or relationship dynamics didn't bother me much. No, what got under my skin were environmental shifts.

I was very territorial—I still am—and I didn't handle changes in the world around me all that well. If my mom rearranged furniture in the living room, I was tense for weeks.

When she remodeled the kitchen, I was grumpy for the entire summer. And when I returned to my tutoring job at the university after summer vacation to find that the supervisor had removed all the cubicles to create a more "spacious, student-friendly environment," I wanted to scream. But instead of looking like a lunatic in front of my coworkers, I retreated to the only place I knew would help me cool my heels: the cemetery just a few blocks from my house. I'd sit in my car by a replica of my favorite statue, La Pieta, and watch the sun set through the trees. Unwittingly, I was seeking refuge in Azrael's vibrations, which, ironically, are those most associated with change.

I'd love to tell you that in doing so, I became a new woman, free of my fear of change. Well, change doesn't bother me much anymore. I've learned from Archangel Cassiel how to just go with the flow and be prepared for anything. I may bristle a bit, but my days of having an intense need to retreat for a week in order to cope with the inevitable are long gone.

You don't have to retreat to a cemetery to connect with Azrael. You can seek his calming qualities through meditating with floral scents or while focusing on smooth, wavy abstracts, or by concentrating your session solely on your crown chakra—your highest chakra—the chakra directly connected to the Source.

Saturday is Azrael's power day. His numerical vibration is zero—not in the Roman numeral sense, but rather in how Egyptians viewed zero: as a symbol of completion rather than a symbol of emptiness. If you're looking to help calm your energies where the fear of death is concerned, keep a small, polished piece of black tourmaline with you. This stone resonates best with Azrael's vibrations, and from a metaphysical perspective, it's said to have soothing, tranquil qualities.

Holidays that best resonate with Azrael: All Souls'/Saints' Day, Fall Equinox, Thanksgiving, Winter Solstice, all holy days of obligation

Best times to channel Azrael's attributes: when entertaining at home (non-holiday); when having dinner for family and friends; when hosting movie night at home; when helping someone deal with loss (any kind of loss, from that of a good friend to a long-standing job); when helping someone go through the grieving/mourning process; when you're in need of ideas to help lift spirits and lighten the mood—just because Azrael is the angel of death doesn't mean he's gloomy!

> *'Tis always best to mind oneself*
> *and keep one's "house" in order.*
> *Trust when I say that you do not want*
> *us archangels to have to pay a visit*
> *and bring to your attention that which*
> *you've been neglecting.*
> *By that point, we're going to tidy things up our way,*
> *and we won't be needing any input from you.*

—ARCHANGEL AZRAEL

Cassiel (Speed of God)

*now there are days when you feel as if Heaven is holding
you back. Well, your life sometimes needs to be put on pause
for a while until everything revolving around it properly
aligns itself so that God's plan may manifest. Hold tight
because oftentimes this can be a long, grueling process that
will demand your patience and determination. Don't give up
on me. There's a reason I'm dragging you through this. All
will be made clear soon enough.*

—ARCHANGEL CASSIEL

Cassiel is one of the most enigmatic angels I've ever met.
There's a reason he doesn't crop up in a lot of angel books:
one of his primary elements is the shadows, and he navigates them with mastery and precision. Hence, not very
many intuitives will encounter him.

When I say that Cassiel is a dark angel, I'm not implying
that he is evil or malevolent in any way. Quite the contrary,
actually. He's a very soft-spoken and reclusive angel who prefers pulling the strings in the background with little or no
input from you. In fact, the less you know of his presence,
the better, in his eyes; but if you're intuitively inclined and
can sense his energies around you, he's not going to suddenly
detect your awareness and then vanish to avoid being seen.
No, if you connect with him, it can be one of the most adventurous times of your life.

Archangel Cassiel is popularly known as the angel of
tears and is the patron of the oppressed and unjustly perse-
cuted, the impoverished and orphans. His heavenly task is
to offer comfort for those enduring extremely burdensome

life trials, and at times he will offer his own strength or even serve as a buffer for the emotional and physical pain some may encounter during particularly difficult life scripts. In fact, Cassiel revealed to me once that the biggest fight he and Archangel Michael ever had was during the trial of Jesus of Nazareth. Angry at feeling helpless, Cassiel wanted to buffer the pain that the soon-to-be Christian savior was enduring. But Michael had very strict and specific orders from Jesus himself not to interfere—no matter what.

"We are eternal. We cannot die. But we can feel pain, and we feel a great deal of it in more ways than humans can ever imagine," Cassiel told me one morning as I was getting ready for work. I was taken aback by the revelation. It seems that even the immortals have burdens to bear in one fashion or another. Cassiel, in particular, seems to shoulder quite a few.

You can invoke Cassiel's energies by focusing on one of his many icons, which include the crow or raven, dragon, full moon, and sword. Grow closer to him by surrounding yourself with the scent of patchouli or musk while meditating in places where his energies are abundant, including old church buildings, cemeteries, or quiet rooftops overlooking the city at night. Autumn, nighttime, and rain showers are some of Cassiel's main elements, so increase your connection with his vibrations by meditating during these times.

Saturday is Cassiel's power day and he rules the planet Saturn, hence making him an angel of karma. His numerical vibration is zero, and stones that best resonate with him are hematite, jasper, kunzite, and pyrite.

If you really want to connect with this angel, who prefers wearing black to any other color and prefers donning leather or denim rather than the typical archangel garb of linen, you can easily do it through rave and techno music—anything digitized or synthesized.

Of all the angels I've ever encountered, I've never met one that had such a strong affinity for a particular part of the world. If you want to immerse yourself in all things Cassiel, just dive headfirst into cultures of the Far East, both ancient and contemporary. When I asked the angel what his favorite foods were, his crystal gray eyes sparkled and he smirked, "Anything cooked in a wok." So there you go. From Eastern philosophy to martial arts, from anime and manga to J-rock and K-pop, have at it. You're sure to encounter an abundance of his vibrations during your explorations.

Holidays that best resonate with Cassiel: Fall Equinox, Lunar New Year, Fall Harvest, Halloween, Winter Solstice

Best times to channel Cassiel's attributes: when dealing with all things related to the military; when meeting with royalty or world leaders; when standing in the position of a martyr (long-suffering, sacrificing); when offering sympathy

I know you're upset and hurting, and that sometimes you may want to be alone for a while, but I hope you don't mind if I stay close. I promise I won't make a lot of noise, make demands, or try to get you to talk about it. Just let me wrap my wings around you. Oh, and it's all right if you feel like crying. My t-shirts are very absorbent.

—ARCHANGEL CASSIEL

Chamuel (Seeker of God)

*If your angelic brothers and sisters have faith in you,
how can you not have faith in yourself?*

—ARCHANGEL CHAMUEL

In Heaven there are many visions of beauty. And though I've only been given brief glimpses of the splendors that await us at home, I have seen enough to say that Archangel Chamuel's garden will take your breath away. Reminiscent of a meticulously kept Japanese garden, it's resplendent with vibrant color. Whenever I pay a visit, I can't help but ease into the tranquil surroundings of flowers, trees, and a winding, bubbly brook.

The garden very much reflects Archangel Chamuel's designation as the patron of nature. He oversees all of Creation and helps to maintain its order and balance. As he does with nature, so he does with our lives. Archangel Chamuel brings to us lessons of healthy living and existing in harmony with our environment, no matter the circumstances. He teaches us how to go within and be the peace we seek in our everyday lives.

I first encountered Chamuel when I was a student in a Buddhist temple. Appearing to me as a Buddhist monk— or sometimes as a Native American shaman—this angel helped me to learn the art of meditation as well as the intuitive healing method of Reiki.

In working with this archangel, I have discovered that the best way to connect with his energies is by keeping nearby his icons of bamboo, the lotus, or a rainstick. Another icon is the stag. Practicing a holistic or Vedic lifestyle can also bring you into alignment with him.

The scents of coconut, ginger, sweet grass, and Nag Champa resonate well with this archangel. His power day is Thursday, so you may find it easier to meditate on this day, especially if you do so in a forest or garden or even up on a hilltop. He's one of the rulers of both Jupiter and Neptune, and his numerical vibration is three.

Archangel Chamuel enjoys the sounds of tribal drums, but a soft flute suits him as well. His favorite sound of all, however, is that of nature.

Connecting with this angel is sure to bring you to a state of relaxing tranquility, so seek him out when you need to unwind and unload daily stress.

Holidays that best resonate with Chamuel: Lunar New Year, Earth Day, Spring Equinox

Best times to channel Chamuel's attributes: when offering care to someone going through a healing stage (physical, mental, emotional, spiritual); when selecting a get-well card; when introducing a new pet to your home or celebrating the arrival of a new pet for someone you know; when caring for a sick pet; when purchasing or moving into a new home

When your meditation garden, your inner place of peace, is being overrun with the weeds of mental clutter, write in your journal to clear your mind of hindering thoughts and your heart of unproductive emotions.

—ARCHANGEL CHAMUEL

Gabriel (God Is My Strength)

*One of the best ways to gauge your potential
and test your skills is to step outside of your comfort zone.
So, would you like to take the initiative, or am I going to
have to drag you? The choice is yours.*

—ARCHANGEL GABRIEL

For an angel that I would not categorize as a warrior angel, Gabriel is perhaps one of the most militant angels I've ever met—even more militant than his brother Michael, the general of the angelic armies.

Archangel Gabriel is the messenger of all messengers. Known as the angel of Annunciation for his role in revealing the birth of Jesus to the Virgin Mary and the arrival of the Messiah to the Three Magi, Gabriel has held a prominent role in Christianity for millennia. He is the angel of communication and the patron of actors, speakers, journalists, commentators, and writers. He also oversees the study of philosophy, mathematics, and physics.

In my past works where I've written about Gabriel, readers have reprimanded me for being too harsh on the angel and painting him in a bad light. Even the angel himself said I've made him out to be too cruel at times. But since day one, I have always said that I depict the angels based on my interactions with them. It's how they appear to me. And while most of my readers agree with me on angels like Michael and Cassiel, Gabriel's fan club has accused me of giving him a bad rap.

Well, if he weren't so darn meticulous and demanding where I'm concerned, maybe I'd have better things to say about the militant angel. I liken him to a spiritual drill sergeant. There's no compromising with the angel. There's no discussion. It's do-or-else with him, and when I see him in a consultation, I usually sigh heavily and tell the client, "My condolences. You have Archangel Gabriel for this leg of your spiritual journey."

And to think, he's the one I went to for help in writing my life script before I was born. Yes, I know I chose him for a reason. I chose him because he's exacting, his attention to detail can't be rivaled, and he's a perfectionist if there ever was one. Perhaps that's why I lock horns with him as much as I do—we're too much alike in that respect. Your encounters with this archangel may be the complete opposite of what I've experienced. In fact, I hope they are. Although Archangel Raphael commissioned me to write my first and second books, Gabriel was the driving force behind them.

Because you've picked up this book, I'm going to assume you're looking for answers to some of life's biggest questions. The moment you start asking is the moment Gabriel will step into your life. Aside from making really important announcements, he is the angel that guides us toward deeper thinking, toward shifting how we perceive the world and ourselves. He's an angel of creativity and thus inspiration, but his approach to inspiring us is by luring us into uncharted territory where we can no longer rely on old ideas and concepts to rescue us. Instead, he works by the saying "Necessity is the mother of all invention." When he tosses us into circumstances where everything tried and true has failed, we're then forced to think outside the box and come up with new ways to approach our circumstances.

I think it's pretty darn brutal on his part, but that's the very human side of me talking. In the grander scheme of things, it's pure genius. Of course it is—he's an angel after all.

"You know you love me," the angel whispered to me one day while I was working on this book. I had been dreading writing about him for weeks, but when he came at me with a smile—a genuine smile—I actually became emotional. In all the years I've known the angel, he's never smiled at me. Not once. Even Archangel Michael has told him some days that he really needs to lighten up, so I was stunned to see such a warm display from him. In that respect, I have to say here that my readers were right. He's not as cold and callous as I have always perceived him to be. And to answer his comment, yes, I do love him. If you're fortunate enough to get his softer side when you connect with him, then you will love him, too.

You can align yourself with Gabriel's energies by focusing on his icons of the trumpet and short sword. Medieval and Renaissance religious artists were highly influenced by this angel, so feel free to indulge with a few prints from Leonardo da Vinci or Michelangelo. Music of church choirs is perfect for connecting with the angel, but Gabriel's energies resonate more with classical European music similar to Catholic hymns. (The foot-stomping, tambourine-pounding, gospel-type music falls more in the domain of Michael or Sandalphon.)

A prime location to connect with Gabriel is just about any place where you can connect with ancient Greek or European Medieval and Renaissance history, such as in a museum, at ancient sites in Greece, at a Renaissance festival, or in old Catholic cathedrals.

I mentioned earlier that angels are not religious, but I don't think anyone would argue that they did inspire religions around the world. Gabriel held much influence over Europe between the thirteenth and seventeenth centuries, a time period that just so happens to coincide with the rise of the Catholic Church. It also coincides with the struggle against the Church by those following the pagan rites and rituals of their ancestors, so meditating on a hill, in the forest, or by a brook by the light of the moon will prove just as beneficial for connecting with Gabriel, especially since the moon falls under his rule.

One thing about Gabriel that I didn't really notice until the writing of this book is his dual nature. Though the angels can take on either gender when appearing to us humans, Gabriel is the only angel that first appeared to me in both his male and female forms. The angel initially appeared to me in his female form not long after my spiritual mentor, Ella, passed away. But because my emotions were still reeling after having lost my mother and then Ella only a couple years apart, I was in no mood for a mothering presence in my life. Gabrielle, as I first called her, realized this and made a quick exit after introducing herself. Later that night, she returned as a he, Gabriel. The only other time I see his female form is with clients.

Gabriel's female form is very gentle, warm, and soft-spoken, whereas his male form is anything but. Then there's his dual influence on the creative mind and the analytical mind, the imagination and knowledge, dreams and the concrete, art and philosophy. He's not a one-trick pony by any means, and if you're someone who is prone to indecision or perhaps warring with different sides of yourself, Archangel Gabriel is definitely an angel who can help bring balance to your internal conflicts.

A few scents that will help you invoke that sense of balance while also aligning you with Gabriel's energies are rose, almond, mint, and sage. Crystals that may help are citrine, azurite, and sapphire.

Monday is Gabriel's power day, and his numerical vibration is three.

Holidays that best resonate with Gabriel: Administrative Professionals Day, Feast of the Annunciation, Christmas, Easter, Mother's Day, Summer Solstice, Winter Solstice

Best times to channel Gabriel's attributes: with anything academic in nature; graduation; a school reunion; a "meet the parents" dinner; when trying to conceive; during pregnancy and childbirth; at a formal dinner party (business), cocktail party, or garden/tea party; at a job interview, promotion, or review; when keeping in touch; casual letter writing

> *When your inner light is shining through,*
> *it's hardly a time to be shy.*
> *Others will like what they see in you,*
> *so move to the front and be noticed!*
>
> —ARCHANGEL GABRIEL

Haniel (Grace of God)

The creative process is often a healing one.

—ARCHANGEL HANIEL

When I first met Haniel, I was taken aback by his radiant light and an overwhelming sense of love and warmth. I was actually on guard at the time I connected with him because I was dealing with issues regarding guilt and self-love. It was another evening of beating myself up over having lost my parents so early in life and wondering what I could have done to be a better daughter for them. That was part of a one-two punch that came with my wishing I could have understood them way back when as deeply as I do now.

"Don't you think for once that they don't love you," the archangel said, appearing out of nowhere. At first I thought he was Raphael, because they resemble each other a bit, but whereas Raphael appears tall and broad-shouldered, Haniel is more slender. The two could pass for twins, but their energy signatures are very different, not to mention Haniel has a devilish smirk that I instantly fell in love with.

When Haniel saw how guarded I was, he flashed a smile and put up his hands, "Calm down, darlin'. I ain't gonna bite ya." Raphael would never use the word "ain't." I knew right then I was dealing with an angel that must have hung around in Michael's circle—with Cassiel, Uriel, Sandalphon, Ariel, and Raziel. Those were the only angels I've ever heard use slang and American colloquialisms. But more than that, Haniel had a slight Southern drawl that didn't seem to really match the angelic robes he was wearing. I didn't say anything to him about how comical I found it, but as he began turning up in client consultations, his clothes began to fit his personality. Suffice it to say that when I see him now, he's all cowboy—not my type at all, which had me wondering why he took on such an appearance around me.

It wouldn't dawn on me until much later, while he was helping me deal with the loss of my parents, that even though he wasn't my type, I was still very comfortable around him and accepting of him. Why? My mother had a special love of action movies, and one of her favorite genres was the western. The Duke, Gregory Peck, and Clint Eastwood were unavoidable in my house on Sundays. If there was a western being televised, she'd find it.

So, who better to bring me messages of love from Mom than someone with enough Southern charm to make ol' Scarlett blush?

As I worked with Haniel, I came to understand him as an angel of mercy and divine love. For a cowboy, he's awfully affectionate, too—always willing to give a hug or to wrap his wings around someone. Polite to the point of addressing clients as "sir" or "ma'am," the angel always makes me smile. So if ever you find yourself battling with guilt or feeling unloved, don't hesitate to seek him out.

Archangel Haniel is the patron of clergy, healers, charity workers, and relief workers. Channeling love directly from the heart of God, this angel helps us to cope with despair and feelings of unworthiness, especially when it comes to being in the presence of the divine. No matter what we may have done—or didn't do—in the past, Haniel brings us the message that God's grace is sufficient and can heal all wounds, even the ones we ourselves may have inflicted.

Some of Haniel's icons are sunbeams, rainbows, and the radiant heart of divine love and compassion. A candlelit lantern, wreaths, and symbols of peace are also associated with the angel and so make great additions to your decor if you're seeking to connect with his energies.

If you're going on a vacation, two notable places where you will find Haniel are America's Southwest, especially around the Grand Canyon, and Australia's Outback. But if you're nowhere near there, you will always find him wherever there are open hearts and helping hands. Donating or volunteering for charity will put you in direct alignment with his compassionate spirit.

Monday and Friday are Haniel's power days, and he co-rules the Moon and Venus. His numerical vibration is five. Stones that resonate best with his energies are jade, rose quartz, and sodalite. When meditating in his direction, you may find the scents of rose and sage useful.

Holidays that best resonate with Haniel: Cinco de Mayo, Fall Equinox, Friendship Day, Valentine's Day

Best times to channel Haniel's attributes: at birthday celebrations; during playful moments of fun and laughter; when you just want to say hello or break the ice; when keeping in touch; when in love or flirting; at a romantic dinner; at engagements and weddings; on a wedding anniversary

Eloquence and the ability to sway the hearts
and minds of people are useful skills to possess
when you need to bring about change.
But more important is the ability to love
and cherish every human being as a child of God.

—ARCHANGEL HANIEL

Iophiel (Beauty of God)

From the wildflower sprouting up through a crack in the concrete to the sunbeam bursting through storm clouds, there is beauty to be found in every facet of your life.

—ARCHANGEL IOPHIEL

Radiant. Beautiful. Exotic. Those are the three words that immediately come to mind whenever anyone mentions Iophiel's name. When I first encountered the archangel, she appeared to me in such a grand manner that I thought her to be the ancient goddess of some civilization long forgotten. Her ample curves were draped in long, flowing robes of pastel green, orange, pink, and yellow. With a seeming mind of their own, they danced and moved about her body in a way that defied the laws of physics. No wind or stray breeze could make cloth flow like that.

Since day one, Iophiel has always held my imagination in thrall. She's bubbly one moment, enchanting the next. Chatty one day, seductively reticent the next. As the archangel of beauty, she lives up to her name. There are times, however, when she seems more like an enchantress than an angel.

Iophiel opens our eyes to the beauty of all Creation and to the beauty we hold within—the light of God, the Holy Spirit itself, the Source. She helps us to recognize the positive in our lives and helps us to think creatively about whatever circumstances we find ourselves in. She is the chief muse of artists and the patron of all things visually creative—painting, sculpture, photography, film, and fashion. She's also Heaven's most social of butterflies, as she's the patron of celebrations and festivals.

Iophiel is an angel full of life, love, and bustling energy, and it's near impossible to remain still when engaging her. You will be moved to do something, even if it's just tapping your toes to a sprightly Irish fiddle or a hopping Cajun accordion. Wherever there is music, people, and food—lots of food—you will most likely find Iophiel.

If you're looking to be moved or inspired by Iophiel's energies, you can look to her icons of the swan and roses. Honeybees and hummingbirds are connected to Iophiel, as well as panthers and tigers. The best places to find her would be art museums, but if that's too dull for your tastes, you can always seek her out at carnivals, festivals, and large flower gardens. If you happen to be traveling and you're looking for a creative boost, you'll find an abundance of Iophiel's energies at all the art hubs throughout the world: Los Angeles, New York, Chicago, New Orleans, Paris, Barcelona, Mumbai, Tokyo, Sydney, and Rio de Janeiro, to name a few. And no, it's not a coincidence that these are also some of the world's largest party hubs as well.

Iophiel's scents cover a broad range, from floral to fresh fruit to homemade dinner. You can invoke her energies by using the scents of carnation, rose, and lilac; apricot, cherry, and orange; or vanilla and cinnamon. One of her favorite stones is pink jade, but she also resonates with opal, rose quartz, and ruby.

Friday is Iophiel's power day, and she co-rules the planets Venus and Saturn. Her numerical vibration is eight, which also symbolizes her perfect female curves.

Holidays that best resonate with Iophiel: All Saints'/Souls' Day, Cinco de Mayo, Kwanzaa, Mardi Gras, Mother's Day, St. Patrick's Day

Best times to channel Iophiel's attributes: at engagements and weddings; at a wedding anniversary or birthday celebration; at festivals and carnivals; at stage and film productions; during a day at the spa; when seeking to increase passion and physical stamina (women); when entertaining at home; at a romantic dinner; at garden/tea parties; at retirement and retirement parties; when selecting a "thinking of you" or "just because" gift

Watch out, walking rainbow comin' through!

—ARCHANGEL MICHAEL
REGARDING IOPHIEL'S CHOICE OF COLORFUL ATTIRE

Metatron (Little Yahweh)

Do not let your heart be troubled, little one.
All of God's heavenly angels are your family,
and we will never abandon you.
We're here, we're listening, and we understand
all that you must endure in this lifetime.
You're not going through this alone, though it may seem so.
We're guiding your every step, so chin up.

—ARCHANGEL METATRON

In Heaven there are massive libraries called the Akashic Records, which contain the logs of everything that has ever transpired in our universe. The name of every being that has come into existence is listed there. Every event that has ever occurred is written in great detail within these large books and scrolls.

I've seen only two sections of the Akashic Records, and that was only after begging for a glimpse of them—it's said that access to the library is by invitation only. In one section, there were large tomes the size of a 1950s Cadillac. The other section levitated in the sky and was made up of walls of what looked to be computer code moving at the speed of light. The maze of walls was endless, and the code was unlike anything I'd ever seen. So, needless to say, my visit to see the Akashic Records didn't provide much spiritual insight because I couldn't read a single word of the divine language they were written in. Still, at least I got a chance to visit with Archangel Metatron, Heaven's chief librarian. Seeing him is always a treat.

Metatron is the patron of children, libraries, teachers, scribes, and record keepers. His icons are books, fluffy white clouds, and rainbows, so don't hesitate to bring his inspirational energies into your child's life by decorating their room accordingly. You can also invoke his love for education and reading through images of the elephant, goose, kitten, or puppy.

Metatron is also a patron of family and togetherness, so align yourself and your family with his energies with scents of lavender, coconut, or anything tropical. The best places to connect with him would be in libraries—naturally. You'll also find his presence strongest during family picnics, especially in large, grassy fields.

Monday is Metatron's power day, and he rules the moon. His numerical vibration is four, and his energies best resonate with crystals of dioptase, moonstone, and topaz or metals of platinum and silver.

Holidays that best resonate with Metatron: Fall Equinox, Father's Day, Teacher's Day

Best times to channel Metatron's attributes: with anything academic; during pregnancy and childbirth; at congratulatory celebrations; at a "meet the parents" dinner; at a dinner with family and friends; at family reunions; at graduation; at a new home; with a new pet; at retirement; during displays of appreciation; when searching for "just because" gifts

Do not discount the praise of your friends and family.
Allow their love and support to be a boost of confidence,
not an anchor of doubt.

—ARCHANGEL METATRON

Michael (Who Is as God)

It never pays to sit and gawk at the superficial
junk in your life, so don't waste time on the trivial.
Focusing instead on what is essential and engaging,
a probing mind will surely lead you to a new self-awareness.
But should that fail, just crank up some music and dance.
In other words, keep moving!

—ARCHANGEL MICHAEL

When one thinks of the biblical archangel that ousted Lucifer and his band of fallen angels from Heaven, the image of a gladiator-type angel might come to mind. Someone strong and fierce. A true warrior angel that could lay waste to any enemy without so much as breaking a sweat. Yes, that's what I always thought Michael to be ... before I met him.

Don't get me wrong, he lives up to his title Master General of the Archangel Armies, but being as there isn't a whole lot of war going on in Heaven, the Master General enjoys sunny days on the beach, volleyball, and surfing whenever he's not out saving us humans from ourselves.

I think that of all the biggest shocks I've had since working with the angels, meeting Michael has to be number one. I was expecting a no-nonsense, military type akin to Achilles. Instead, I got a football-loving, tailgating, pizza-chomping disco junkie. With a smile warm enough to melt the polar ice caps, Michael is full of fun, humor, wit, and sarcasm. His laughter is contagious, and when he appears at the forefront of our lives, it's to tell us to relax and try not to take things too seriously. His message is not only for us humans, but for his angelic brothers as well. I've lost count of how many times he's told Gabriel and Uriel to "just chill."

The most beloved and most beautiful angel in Heaven is the patron of sports and fitness, sports cars, dancers, law enforcement, and the military. You can connect with his sunny energies through his icons of the lion, eagle, sword and shield, and battle flag. But if you really want to give your courage a bit of a boost, just go outside on a sunny day. Michael rules the sun, and sunbathing is one of his favorite pastimes in his human form. So load up the cooler and head to the beach with some friends. When the sun goes down, you can still keep the Michael momentum going by starting a bonfire. If there's one thing the angel loves as much as sunbathing, it's eating. Toasting marshmallows and a midnight game of volleyball is the perfect way to infuse your soul with his radiant energy.

If you can't make it to the beach, then stay at home and crank the music. Michael loves dancing to rock, pop, disco, soul, reggae, hip hop, and gospel. Anything with a fast beat is right up his alley. The point is to *move*. Michael never sits still for long. He is constantly on the go, so the best way to conjure up vibrations similar to his is to be like him. Physical exercise, dancing, bike riding, or just a casual Sunday drive are all great ways to connect.

Sunday is Michael's power day, and he co-rules the Sun and Mars. His numerical vibrations are one and three. Stones that best resonate with this angel are carnelian, cat's eye, emerald, garnet, and sunstone.

Holidays that best resonate with Michael: Armed Forces Day, Cinco de Mayo, Easter, Independence Day, Kwanzaa,

Mardi Gras, Memorial Day, Summer Solstice, Veterans Day

Best times to invoke Michael's energies: a day at the beach; a day at the game; at a tailgating party; at Sunday dinner; at a backyard picnic; on movie night; at breakfast or brunch; during fun activities; when wishing someone good luck; with anything involving the military; when showing or encouraging patriotism; at a school reunion; when engaging in sports and competitions; when seeking to increase passion and physical stamina (men)

If you're going to lead, lead.
But know that honor, integrity, and rationality are not optional weapons to carry in your arsenal.

—ARCHANGEL MICHAEL

Raguel (Friend of God)

You may have the ambition. You may have the drive.
But racing through life with pride as your passenger will
cause you to burn out every time.
Don't shun a helping hand.
Every champion racer needs a good pit crew
to keep him on the tracks.

—ARCHANGEL RAGUEL

Always on the move, Archangel Raguel is the go-between for the Source and just about everyone else in Heaven. Whereas Gabriel is God's messenger to humans, Raguel is God's messenger to the Heavenly Hosts. At one time I called him God's secretary, but the intensely serious angel bristled at that analogy. He didn't seem too indignant when I likened him to a department manager, however. Who says angels can't have egos?

Archangel Raguel is the patron of labor, industry, agriculture, and community. In his book, there is no time for play.

"One must be dedicated and focused when it comes to whatever task is delegated to her," he says. Because Raguel is always on the go, it's sometimes difficult to pin the angel down for insight or wisdom. Luckily, he economizes both time and words, so if you do get a chance to connect and speak with him, his input will always be concise. You'll get no water-cooler chitchat out of him.

If you find yourself low on energy or feeling unmotivated, you can channel Raguel's high-octane characteristics by surrounding yourself with icons and images that are often associated with him, such as books, a quill and ink, the roadrunner, orchards, and vegetable gardens.

You can align yourself with this angel by staying in motion. Meditation through tai chi, yoga, or other forms of physical exercise are powerful ways to connect, along with utilizing the scent of hickory. Infuse your living space with energies that resonate with Raguel by placing stones of amazonite, gold calcite, and smoky quartz nearby. Adding various shades of blue to your decor will help as well. While blue is known for being a relaxing color, it is Raguel's favorite color and hence will also lend you that extra boost of energy when you keep the angel in your thoughts.

Raguel's power day is Wednesday, and he co-rules the planets Mercury and Uranus. His numerical vibration is two.

Holidays that best resonate with Raguel: Administrative Professionals Day, Fall Equinox, National Boss Day, Tax Day

Best times to channel Raguel's attributes: when going through a divorce or breakup; at a formal business dinner; at a job interview, review, or promotion; with legal matters; when growing a garden; during the fall harvest

Don't be afraid of success.
You worked too hard to get to this point
to throw it all away.
Believe in yourself.

—ARCHANGEL RAGUEL

Ramiel (God's Mercy)

Make sure that everything you build in life begins
with a solid foundation.
Your sense of responsibility and hard work
will not go unrewarded.

—ARCHANGEL RAMIEL

In the immeasurable library called the Akashic Records, Archangel Metatron is in good company when it comes to maintaining a log of every life ever lived. Archangel Ramiel is Metatron's assistant, but he's a bit of a loner. If there was ever an angel I could consider strange in his demeanor, it would be Ramiel, with his fixation on time and the law of causality. The angel is always poring over old logs, gazing at the stars, or tinkering with one of his many timepieces. He finds humanity fascinating, though he's admitted that even after the countless millennia since we came to be, he still can't quite figure us out.

Archangel Ramiel is the patron of historians, archeologists, librarians, museum curators, and just about any profession that involves the study of cultures and human behavior. He's not much of a hands-on angel when it comes to interacting with humans. He prefers working in the background and lending us wisdom and insight by showing us patterns in our lives that could use some adjusting for better spiritual growth.

If you find yourself at a point in your life where you're saying, "Hey, wait a minute. I've been through this exact same situation before," you can look to Ramiel to help pinpoint the lessons you may have missed the last time you encountered a similar challenge. His icons are the calendar, hourglass, and sundial, and you can best align yourself with his energies by visiting old libraries and historical museums. Working in a flower garden is always a great way to connect as well.

When you feel that looking into your past could help you understand where you may be headed in the future, you're definitely aligned with Ramiel, so keep a journal of your thoughts and theories. Doing so will invoke the energies of this archangel and will help you to think about your life and yourself in new, insightful ways.

Meditating on Ramiel's power day of Thursday may prove useful, especially if you infuse your space with a sweet scent like vanilla or honey. Gemstones of alexandrite and sodalite best resonate with this angel, along with earth tones. His numerical vibrations are two and five, and he rules the planet Jupiter.

Holidays that best resonate with Ramiel: Administrative Professionals Day, Fall Equinox, Grandparents Day, Spring Equinox, Summer Solstice, Winter Solstice

Best times to channel Ramiel's attributes: with anything academic in nature; at a job interview, review, or promotion; when researching history, ancestry, or genealogy

> *Be bold and open to expressing yourself*
> *in new and creative ways.*
> *Graciousness with a touch of ambition*
> *can open many doors of opportunity for you.*

—ARCHANGEL RAMIEL

Raphael (God Heals)

There are no should haves or could haves.
All that exists is what is.

—ARCHANGEL RAPHAEL

As you read in earlier chapters, my battle with health issues has been long and arduous. I've been in and out of hospitals for so long that I feel I've put in more time than most successful doctors. But what's kept me sane—as far as health is concerned, anyhow—is the presence of my good friend Archangel Raphael. When a sudden pain hits or I've been feeling more under the weather than usual, his name is the first I call, and never, not once, has he failed to appear by my side when I was in need of comfort.

Raphael is the archangel of healing. I often call him the "gentle giant" because he appears to me as taller than the other archangels. With broad shoulders that he drapes in white, blue, or purple robes, his presence gives me a sense of peace and great security. In the beginning, however, it wasn't always so. When I had my first health crisis, he was the first angel I called upon and the last one I listened to. It was a time of anger and great confusion on my part, but never did he chastise me for it. In fact, he simply remained close by while keeping a silent yet unrelenting watch over me.

Oftentimes I fell asleep in his arms. Sometimes I awoke to his radiant features gazing down at me. He was the first angel that I commissioned a drawing for, and for the seven years that I lived in a single bedroom, that artwork hung over my bed. It was comforting to know he was near, especially when the pain became unbearable. So many nights I clutched my sheets as I sobbed in agony, when in my intuitive eye I was clutching his robes, begging him to never abandon me, begging him to make all the pain go away, be it physical, emotional, or mental. The beautiful angel of mercy that he is, he wiped away my tears, soothed my feverish aches, and lulled me into peaceful rest when all my tried-and-true methods had failed.

To say he lives up to his duty as the angel of healing is an understatement.

Archangel Raphael is the patron of healers, light workers, the medical field, stargazers, and travelers. The dolphin, shepherd's crook, and white dove are some of his icons, but he's also associated with dreamcatchers, the hare, the unicorn, fairies, enchanted forests, and the oceans.

You can align yourself with Raphael's energies by infusing your space with his scents of frankincense and myrrh, lavender, and sage, or by keeping gemstones of amethyst, lapis lazuli, or turquoise nearby.

Places where you'll find Raphael's presence the strongest are near bodies of water, in forests, and in mountainous regions. The dreamscape is also one of his favorite dwelling places.

Wednesday is Raphael's power day, and he rules the planet Mercury. His numerical vibration is the number six.

Holidays that best resonate with Raphael: Earth Day, Nurses Day, All Souls'/Saints' Day, Thanksgiving, Winter Solstice, all holy days of obligation

Best times to channel Raphael's attributes: when traveling; when invoking blessings; when offering care to others; when showing concern or sympathy; when sending someone a get-well gift; when celebrating a new home or pet; during a day at the spa

> *When pondering how best to deal*
> *with some of life's most pressing circumstances,*
> *there will always come a time when you must*
> *separate the wheat from the chaff.*
> *This is to say that you must evaluate*
> *what has true value to you and must be kept,*
> *and what has long served its purpose and must be discarded.*

—ARCHANGEL RAPHAEL

Raziel (God's Secret)

Sometimes you have to explore the darker places within in order to understand where light shines the brightest. So acknowledge any ill feelings that may assail you from time to time. Write them down and get them out of your system so the fertile foundation of your soul can better nurture your brighter side. Never berate yourself. Learn from your errors and move on.

—ARCHANGEL RAZIEL

Irreverent and sharp-tongued, Archangel Raziel, or Raz, as everyone calls him, can be a bit of a handful to humans and fellow archangels alike. As a keeper of secrets, he has the uncanny ability to say a lot without saying much of anything—an ability that has been known to drive Master General Michael to the point of distraction. There aren't many vault keepers, as it were. I've only come across two, Archangels Raziel and Iophiel, and both are as different as night and day.

Where Archangel Iophiel is so bright and cheery that you can see her coming from miles away, Raziel can be standing right behind you and you'd never know it. Like Archangel Cassiel, Raz is a master of the shadows, and it is through them that he navigates his way in and out of human lives. I'd like to reiterate that just because an angel is dark in demeanor does not in any way denote that he is evil or malevolent— quite the contrary. Raziel may be associated with things that most of the Western world considers dark or macabre, but his purpose is to enlighten seekers and guide them along spiritual paths that lead to profound insight.

This angel tends to work in the background, hidden from human view, but should you encounter him, expect to have one heck of an adventure. He's the master of slang and contemporary colloquialisms. He also has a fondness for this particular reality and all the fun toys we have, like sports cars and motorbikes.

This angel loves speed.

Archangel Raziel is the patron of prophets, mysteries, alchemy, and metaphysics, just to name a few. His icons are daggers, smoke, keys, and key rings, along with masks and veils. Other associations are the fox, scorpion, and spider, as well as cloaks, codes, locks, and vaults.

You can align yourself with Raziel's energies by bringing any number of his icons into your personal space or by losing yourself in a good book of mystery and intrigue (fiction or nonfiction). Scents that best resonate with this angel are woodsy, smoky scents, so incense of cedar, pine, or sweet grass is always a great way to infuse your aura with energies similar to his. While you're at it, it wouldn't hurt to carry a stone of hematite, jet, obsidian, or smoky quartz with you.

Wednesday is Raziel's power day, and he rules the planet Neptune. His numerical vibration is zero. Unlike Azrael, where zero represents completion, the zero associated with Raziel represents void and emptiness, as well as chaos.

Holidays that best resonate with Raziel: April Fools' Day, Fall Harvest, Fall Equinox, Halloween, Winter Solstice

Best times to channel Raziel's attributes: when being entrusted with a secret; when writing in a private diary; when hiding something of value to you; when investigating a mystery

Not all acts of sacrifice will be rewarded with
acknowledgment or praise, so don't seek it.
Stay humble. Heaven is watching. That's all that matters.

—ARCHANGEL RAZIEL

Sandalphon (Brother)

Let your inner light illuminate the path before you and know
that regardless of any missteps you think you may have
made, you'll still arrive exactly where you need to be.

—ARCHANGEL SANDALPHON

"So, how would you like a baby brother?" God asked Archangel Michael one day.

"Say huh?" Nonplussed, the Master General glanced up suddenly with the funniest look of befuddlement on his face. At least, that's Gabriel's retelling of the moment when Sandalphon, as we now know him, came to be.

This archangel is a baby in the angel family, being as he was born after the creation of Earth. In fact, he's only one of two documented humans who, because of their pure and pious hearts, were allowed to bypass death and were taken straight up into Heaven. Those two humans would be the biblical figures of Enoch and Elijah—Metatron and Sandalphon, respectively.

While Metatron has retained much of his age—that is to say his energies give off the air of someone who is old and wise—Sandalphon traded in his beard and walking stick for a much more youthful presence. Of all the archangels I interact with on a regular basis, he by far appears as one of the youngest. On average, the archangels look to be in their late twenties to early thirties, but Sandalphon—whom I've dubbed the "Peter Pan of Heaven"—is the face of eternal youth, along with his even younger-looking sister Ariel.

Wide-eyed and rosy-cheeked, this angel can often be found stepping on the heels of his big brother, Michael. I've seen the two go at each other much like human brothers would. They wrestle, fight, and call each other silly names, but what I adore so much about seeing them together is the radiant love between them. There's nothing quite like it. There's nothing Michael wouldn't do for Sandalphon, except allow the youthful angel to go into battle. While Sandalphon can most likely hold his own against any foe, Michael keeps his young sibling on the sidelines. I've never been told why, and Sandalphon tends to pout when the topic arises, but I'm going to take a guess that it has to do with Sandalphon's position as the angel of love. He's not a warrior angel by any stretch of the imagination, but that's not to say that he's any less powerful than his archangel siblings. Sandalphon's powers of love and imagination are unrivaled and should never be taken lightly.

Archangel Sandalphon is the patron of children, academics, charity, music, games, and love, just to name a few. His icons are the harp, candy, gifts, and baseball. Other associations include amusement parks, schools, marching bands, playgrounds, and children's toys.

You'll always find an abundance of Sandalphon's energies in sunlit, grassy fields, at a baseball field, in beds of wildflowers, on hay rides, and at natural labyrinths—you know, those really cool mazes made up of either meticulously trimmed shrubbery or stacked bales of hay.

Sweet scents of blueberry, pineapple, strawberry, or classic bubblegum invoke this angel's energies, along with that of freshly mowed grass.

Being as Sandalphon is Heaven's resident muse when it comes to music, playing his favorite genres—jazz, big band, blues, bluegrass, '50s rock, and teen pop—will align your aura with his and fill your thoughts with visions of him. Like Archangel Michael, Sandalphon loves to dance, so crank the volume and shake a tail feather with him.

Friday is Sandalphon's power day, and he rules the planet Venus. Gemstones of blue tourmaline and fluorite best resonate with him, and his numerical vibration is seven.

Holidays that best resonate with Sandalphon: April Fools' Day, Christmas, Friendship Day, Halloween, New Year's Day, Spring Equinox, Sweetest Day, Valentine's Day

Best times to channel Sandalphon's attributes: with anything of an academic nature; at birthdays; when offering congratulations or giving a congratulatory speech; during a day at the game (all sports, especially children's); when entertaining at home; at Sunday dinner; at backyard picnics; with anything involving healthy fun and laughter; at graduation; on test/examination day; when you just want to say hello or break the ice; when in love or flirting; when sending messages of "missing you"; when showing love and appreciation

> *Charitable acts will fill your heart with joy*
> *and elevate your soul to new heights.*
>
> —ARCHANGEL SANDALPHON

Uriel (Fire of God)

Yes, I'm aware that obstacles may block you
from where you want to go.
They're put there on purpose.
Why? Because the path you're trying to take
is not the path you are destined to travel.
Stand down and look inward. I will reveal to you the path
you are to take when the time is right.
Until then, patience is your friend.

—ARCHANGEL URIEL

As with Archangel Gabriel, readers have rallied behind Archangel Uriel and accused me of being too hard on the angel.

"Hey, he's not as bad as you make him out to be."

Perhaps I'm just the unluckiest angel medium on the planet, because I've only seen Archangel Uriel in two moods: brooding and cynical. Even other archangels steer clear of this fiery angel—on his *good* days. Michael tends to ignore his brother's acerbic attitude toward humans, but I've seen Sandalphon slowly shrink and hide behind the Master General whenever the angel of the Apocalypse shows up.

Is that to say that we humans should steer clear of Uriel? Absolutely not. Even with his perpetual dour mood, I still adore him with all my heart. After all, he's the patron of prophets, visionaries, lawmakers, and seekers of the truth. If you have a cause that involves keeping people informed or uncovering the truth for the common good of all, then Uriel is the one you want in your corner. But beware, this archangel detests hypocrisy, so don't cast the first stone unless you know without a doubt that you yourself aren't guilty, too.

I tend to call Uriel the angel of conscience—that voice that reprimands you for doing something you know you shouldn't, be it cheating on your diet or not telling the cashier that she gave you too much change back. He's the voice that whispers in our ear, urging us to always do the right thing and to think of others, not just ourselves.

I know that in my earlier books I painted Uriel as abrasive and difficult to approach, but as my relationship with him has deepened, I've come to appreciate his presence in my life more and more. Between him and Gabriel, I've come to understand how important discipline is in my life. While I'm the first to say I have no willpower in some areas, like eating, I'm not as quick to jump to conclusions as I was during my younger years. Also, I am no longer one to jump to anger the moment things don't go my way.

So many times when I find myself ready to launch into a huge tirade about something I'm passionate about, I'll hear Uriel or Gabriel whisper, "This isn't your fight. Let it go." Because of them, I'm able to take things in stride … most days. Long ago, that wasn't always the case. When you're unsure if you should speak up or stand down for something you believe in, look in Uriel's direction. He'll let you know when it's your turn to act or when it's something you should simply let God handle.

You can align yourself with Uriel's energies by adding images of his icons to your surroundings—bow and arrow, chariot, or the scales of justice. Other items associated with this fiery angel are the phoenix, boar, bullwhip, volcanoes, and lightning.

Uriel resonates best with fiery or spicy scents like cinnamon, nutmeg, and pepper. If you want to invoke his energies, you can wear accessories made of gold with stones of Apache tears, jet, or obsidian. To best connect with Uriel, candlelight, a campfire, or even a fire in the fireplace are good ways to set the atmosphere, along with using the colors gold, orange, or red.

Uriel's power day is Tuesday, and he rules the planet Mars. His numerical vibration is nine.

Holidays that best resonate with Uriel: Armed Forces Day, Fall Equinox, Independence Day, Spring Equinox, Summer Solstice, Tax Day, Veterans Day, Winter Solstice

Best times to channel Uriel's attributes: during a day at the game; when enduring a divorce or breakup; with all legal matters; with anything pertaining to the military

For your own sake,
forgive.

—ARCHANGEL URIEL

Zadkiel (Righteousness of God)

One day, you'll awaken to the realization
that your greatest masterpiece is you.

—ARCHANGEL ZADKIEL

Fatherly and gentle in his demeanor, Archangel Zadkiel is an angel of mercy that helps us come to terms with God's love for us. When we battle with feelings of unworthiness, guilt, depression, or other forms of internal torment, Zadkiel brings to us the message of just how important we are as children of God.

The one interesting characteristic I've noticed about this archangel is that he often appears to me as much older than the other archangels I've connected with. While most of the angels appear to be in their late teens to early thirties, Zadkiel appears to be much older. Don't think that he's some crabby old guy hobbling along with a walking stick. No, Zadkiel may appear as a man in his late sixties, but his well-muscled build gives off the air that he can kick just as much butt as Master General Michael.

I believe that the reason Zadkiel has often appeared to myself and others in this fashion is to reinforce his angelic position as being that of a wise sage that is always willing to take us under his wing. He provides a great sense of security when he is near, and I have found in my interactions with hundreds of clients that he draws closest to those who have either lacked a father figure in their childhood or have had troubled relationships with their father. A gentle angel who exudes nothing but love and compassion, Zadkiel teaches us that we must learn to love ourselves as God loves us—unconditionally.

Archangel Zadkiel is the patron of ministers, philanthropists, saints, and prisoners, among others. His icons are similar to those of Archangel Raphael: books, the dove, and the shepherd's crook. But you can differentiate between the angels, no matter how they may appear to you, by noting the color of their auras. Raphael tends to work with darker shades of blue, purple, and burgundy, whereas Zadkiel tends to work with light blues, greens, and white. I have seen the forests in both Raphael's and Zadkiel's mansions. Raphael's seems to be locked at dusk with a dark yet colorful sky of violet, orange, and deep red. Zadkiel's is always sunlit, warm, and airy. These two are very loving and compassionate and have very distinct tastes.

You can connect with Archangel Zadkiel by adding a few of his associations to your personal space—images of the gourd, the peach, a jeweled chalice, or the planet Jupiter, which he rules. Artwork in bronze, copper, or iron depicting the angel's icons and associations is a wonderful way to invoke his energies, as well as the placement of stones such as amethyst, jade, and kunzite.

Zadkiel's power day is Thursday, his numerical vibration is seven, and his energies can be best felt during the spring season. While meditating, try using the scent of peach, rosemary, or sweet floral to infuse your space and help align yourself with this benevolent angel.

Holidays that best resonate with Zadkiel: Armed Forces Day, Earth Day, Father's Day, Grandparents Day, Spring Equinox

Best times to channel Zadkiel's attributes: when sending notes or gifts of congratulations; during the fall harvest; at retirement

Embrace fully each moment of harmony you create,
and allow those close to you to encourage and inspire you
to maintain your current momentum. Surrounding yourself
with vibrant, youthful energy will give you just the right
amount of vigor you need.

—ARCHANGEL ZADKIEL

BIBLIOGRAPHY

Andrews, Ted. *Animal-Speak*. St. Paul, MN: Llewellyn Publications, 2008.

Biggs, Matthew, Jekka McVicar, and Bob Flowerdew. *Vegetables, Herbs and Fruit: An Illustrated Encyclopedia*. New York: Firefly Books, 2008.

Browne, Sylvia. *Life on the Other Side: A Psychic's Tour of the Afterlife*. New York: New American Library, 2000.

Bunson, Matthew. *Angels A to Z: A Who's Who of the Heavenly Host*. New York: Three Rivers Press, 1996.

Cunningham, Scott. *Cunningham's Encyclopedia of Magical Herbs*. St. Paul, MN: Llewellyn Publications, 2008.

Davidson, Gustav. *A Dictionary of Angels: Including the Fallen Angels*. New York: The Free Press, 1967.

Davis, Patricia. *Aromatherapy: An A–Z: The Most Comprehensive Guide to Aromatherapy Ever Published*. London: Random House, 2005.

Duin, Julia. "Half of Americans Believe in Guardian Angels." *Washington Times*, September 19, 2008, http://www.washingtontimes.com/news/2008/sep/19/half-of-americans-believe-in-angels.

Eason, Cassandra. *The Illustrated Directory of Healing Crystals.* London: Collins & Brown, 2003.

Embree, Ainslie. *Sources of Indian Tradition.* New York: Columbia University Press, 1988.

Guiley, Rosemary. *The Encyclopedia of Saints.* New York: Checkmark Books, 2001.

Keel, Othmar, and Christopher Uehlinger. *Gods, Goddesses, and Images of God.* London: T&T Clark Publishers, 2001.

Lerma, John, MD. *Into the Light.* Franklin Lakes, NJ: Career Press, 2007.

Lewis, James R., and Dorothy Oliver. *Angels A to Z.* Canton, MI: Visible Ink Press, 2002.

Martin, Richard P. *Myths of the Ancient Greeks.* New York: The Penguin Group, 2003.

Moody, Raymond A. Jr., MD. *Life After Life.* New York: HarperCollins, 2001.

Myss, Caroline, PhD. *Anatomy of the Spirit.* New York: Three Rivers Press, 1996.

Simpson, Liz. *The Book of Chakra Healing.* New York: Sterling Publishing, 1999.

Taylor, Terry Lynn. *Messengers of Light: The Angels' Guide to Spiritual Growth.* Tiburon, CA: H. J. Kramer, Inc., 1990.

Turner, Patricia, and Charles Russell Coulter. *Dictionary of Ancient Deities*. New York: Oxford University Press, 2000.

Virtue, Doreen, PhD. *Archangels & Ascended Masters*. Carlsbad, CA: Hay House, 2003.

To Write to the Author

If you wish to contact the author or would like more information about this book, please write to the author in care of Llewellyn Worldwide Ltd. and we will forward your request. Both the author and publisher appreciate hearing from you and learning of your enjoyment of this book and how it has helped you. Llewellyn Worldwide Ltd. cannot guarantee that every letter written to the author can be answered, but all will be forwarded. Please write to:

Chantel Lysette
℅ Llewellyn Worldwide
2143 Wooddale Drive
Woodbury, MN 55125-2989

Please enclose a self-addressed stamped envelope for reply, or $1.00 to cover costs. If outside the U.S.A., enclose an international postal reply coupon.